SOLOING

"As the environment of most large institutions becomes more and more toxic to human values and health, we all have to wonder if the 'end of the job' isn't just around the corner. But what will replace this icon of the Industrial Age? Self-employment? Freelancing? Harriet Rubin suggests a very different image, soloing. In so doing, she may have hit upon the workplace metaphor for the Post-Industrial world"

—Peter Senge

"The number of Americans leaving the corporate world to go it alone is swelling to a huge wave. This wise and supremely instructive book is all you will need to make the transition."

—John Naisbitt, author of *Megatrends*

"Harriet Rubin has clicked into the trend we call Cashing Out: 'The essence of the American dream today: no boss, no red tape… working the hours you want, working with the clients you choose…' If you have a dream so strong that the thought of not doing it makes you really unhappy, then have the courage of your convictions: Read this book."

—Faith Popcorn, Faith Popcorn's Brain Reserve

"A wonderful read and a great road map for discovering that you are who you are—not what you do"

—Frederic D. Rosen,
founder and builder of Ticketmaster and current Soloist

Harriet Rubin, founder of Doubleday's Currency imprint, is a flourishing soloist. She works with leading CEOs to define and deepen their visionary objectives. A contributing editor to *Fast Company,* she is also the author of the bestseller *The Princessa: Machiavelli for Women,* and the founder of www.ivillage.com/TheSoloist (AOL key-word: ivillage) She lives in New York City.

Also by Harriet Rubin:

The Princessa: Machiavelli for Women

SOLOING

Realizing Your
Life's Ambition

Harriet Rubin

RANDOM HOUSE
BUSINESS BOOKS

First published in the UK in 2000 by Random House Busines Books,
Random House, 20 Vauxhall Bridge Road, London SW1V 2SA

Random House Australia (Pty) Limited
20 Alfred Street, Milsons Point
Sydney, New South Wales 2061, Australia

Random House New Zealand Limited
18 Poland Road, Glenfield
Auckland 10, New Zealand

Random House (Pty) Limited
Endulini, 5a Jubilee Road, Parktown 2193, South Africa

The Random House Group Limited Reg. No. 954009

Papers used by Random House are natural, recyclable products made from
wood grown in sustainable forests. The manufacturing processes conform to
the environmental regulations of the country of origin.

ISBN 0 09 941022 2

Companies, institutions and other organizations wishing to make bulk
purchases of books published by Random House should contact their
local bookstore or Random House direct:

Special Sales Director
Random House, 20 Vauxhall Bridge Road, London SW1V 2SA
Tel 0207 840 8470   Fax 0207 828 6681

www.randomhouse.co.uk
businessbooks@randomhouse.co.uk

Printed and bound in Great Britain by, Bookmarque Ltd, Croydon, Surrey

For my father
Bernard Rubin
(1912–1977):
soloist.

Contents

PART II: THE BUSINESS OF BEING YOURSELF

Preface

This is a book about a journey of the spirit. When I first met Harriet Rubin, we were both executives in our respective industries. She was the publisher of Currency, an important division of Doubleday Publishing Company, and I was a vice president of Intel Corp. Three years later, she stepped out of that "role" to become the CEO of her own life. It took me three years more to follow suit. After twenty years as an industry executive, I have just become the CEO of a company that has only one employee, me!

This is a guide to the joy of freedom and its cost. It is written by someone who took the risk of casting off a corporate identity to become herself. Many of us are trapped by success. We work so hard to achieve a certain position proving ourselves over and over to a succession of bosses and bosses of bosses. While we may be frustrated with the bureaucracy of our companies, we are also comforted by the structure they provide. We know we are capable of more and blame the system for limiting our abilities. Yet it is our own fears that limit us. In starting one of the most important journeys in my life, this book is my guide.

I invite you to take this journey, a trip to yourself. My guess is that when you arrive you will ask why you did not leave earlier. I know I did.

Avram Miller
RECENT VP OF INTEL, CEO OF HIS OWN LIFE

Part I INVENT YOURSELF

Definition

1. Your Work Was Your Life. Now Let Your Life Be Your Work

"Solo" for me conjures up images of adventurers who never hyperventilate: Charles Lindbergh, who risked his life flying across the Atlantic in a tin plane of the strength tuna is packed in today. Or Reinhold Messner, called the Michael Jordan of alpinists—accurate if Jordan faced death climbing Everest alone and without oxygen. Or Billie Holiday, wanting "to get all the feeling, eat all the good foods, experience every experience, and sing," so she could revise the sound of the blues for all who came after her. When I walked out of the organisation I'd served for ten years—determined not to manage or lead any living creature, not even a dog on a leash—I didn't think I had anything in common with those brave souls. I wasn't exactly walking off a cliff into some frightful new dimension. But in fact, I was. It was a dangerous, cold, and very lonely walk off a cliff called Security. It was worth the trip. In Solo Land, work and freedom are synonyms, not opposites. When I got over the fear, I felt something of the thrill that lured those great adventurers to the brink: the sheer aliveness of believing in myself and what I was doing enough to do it solo.

I'm the last person in the world who ever should have had the guts or the need to leave the corporation. I grew up dirt-poor, so I was eternally grateful for my paycheck. I loved organisational life. I celebrated it by starting a business books company at Doubleday in 1989. I was not only a citizen of the corporate world, I promoted its ideas by publishing such best-selling authors as Peter Senge, Andy Grove, Faith Popcorn, and Don Peppers. I was a success. I didn't have to leave. Most days I didn't want to leave. I liked the oatmeal in the company cafeteria.

And yet, the routine was beginning to get to me. Though I was publisher of my own imprint, I had authority over nothing. Not even paper stock. A good book went to press and came out looking like "beaver lick"—if a beaver licked it, the paper would dissolve—because "quality" systems demanded the cheapest possible paper that would still hold ink. This was the profit machine I had to keep feeding, at the expense of my own reputation. I began to wonder, why?

I had no answer until a Buddhist monk came to see me. We were talking about a book he might write, when he suddenly asked: "What do you do when you reach the top of a forty-foot pole?" When I worked in publishing, I had a ready answer for everything. "You climb back down and look for another pole," I said. Silence. "I mean you relax and enjoy the view. No, wait. You think about how you got into that position in the first place." The monk was packing up his interest in me. "I've got it!" I shouted. "You dial 911." He changed the conversation. I realized I'd been saying "you" as if he'd asked the question about some third party. The monk was asking about me. I'd reached the top of the pole of publishing, something he saw more clearly than I.

There was something worse than topping-out: Forty feet wasn't a height to be at all proud of.

Some riddles demand doing, not thinking, to solve them. By the time I left Doubleday three years after this visit, I knew that at the top of the pole, you keep on climbing without a ladder, without a prop. Climbing with a ladder is hard. Climbing without a ladder is harder. It's exhilarating. It's soloing.

I left because I wanted more and I thought I might actually have a shot at getting it. I left because I was tired of telling bosses and clients, "You're right," when I

7

knew they were wrong. I left because I got to be so good at serving, I thought: "Why not serve me?" So I walked out. SOLO. I was free for the first time in, well, my whole life! I had no appointments, no boss, no corporate politics, no pasted-on smile. I came to believe that everything I'd published about managing and leading was a lie. Corporations, for all their vaunted systems of management, weren't exactly turning out great work. That's what I wanted to try my hand at. To do great work, you couldn't be responsible for anyone but you. That was the only way to be honest to yourself, and to test yourself to the core. To do important work, thrilling work, you had to go it alone. Same as an artist.

Soloing is a lot like being an artist. Soloing demands creativity. Self-discipline. Self-leadership. An ability to see the world in a grain of sand, because your span of control shrinks, but your power to influence others expands. Most of all, soloing demands courage: the gumption to be opinionated and stand up for your own visions. This last is not as easy as it sounds.

One image beckoned me like an oasis: the image of Picasso grinding up lapis and sapphires to make the haunting blue paint of his famous blue period. He stretched his own canvases. He locked himself in a basement workroom to create pictures of his own imagination. He left for an absinthe when he wanted and came back when the visions in his mind drove him to make

8

something of the sapphire blue and the stark white canvas. I wanted to touch my work with that kind of testing intimacy. I wanted to see if I could make a success of myself on my own terms, not by anybody else's rules. I wanted to believe work could be more than a four-letter word. I knew it was for some.

But I was months away from absinthes or the blue of sky and dreams, or the life of an artist. When I walked out of the Ze Tower, as we called Doubleday headquarters because the skyscraper seemed like the place you'd take an innocent bride and cut off her head, I felt beheaded—or was that just lightheaded?—walking around the goal-oriented Manhattanites like a bit of a freak. I had no idea where to go next on that bright Friday when the world stretched out before me like an endless weekend. I was floating on a magic carpet. I didn't have to be anywhere. Whom do you belong to when you belong nowhere? Who are you when you leave?

I didn't know where my next job would be coming from. My expertise was in publishing books, but my solo dream was to write them and consult, speechify, and study. I didn't know if I could do any of these dream jobs. I didn't have any contacts in these fields who trusted me to deliver on my promises. I was scared. To some extent, it was great to feel anything for a change, even fright.

Then I looked down. I was out on a limb. Except for

a handful of people who'd left big companies and disappeared soon after, no one I really knew had made the trip before me. Where was everybody? Was I suddenly with them, lost among the ghosts?

UH OH

There is a lot of advice available for people who take another job, for people who leave to start up a company, even for people who decide to loaf and travel. But there was nothing for the soloist. I had no guide to prepare me for the disorienting experiences ahead.

When I think back to that time, I remember feeling so totally alone that I took to calling AT&T at dinnertime to query *them* about their One Rate Plan. It was often the one conversation of the day. My first week out, I felt like some little gutter girl, watching people step right over me as they headed into big fancy restaurants in their big fancy clothes. I had become so small they didn't even have to push me aside to clear the sidewalk. I just blew away under the sound of their laughter. On the one hand, I was happy to have given up the superficial life of dinners on an expense account that had no limit. Goodbye to the maitre d's who kissed my hand because it held company plastic. And yet, I wondered if I would ever eat off a white tablecloth again with all that cutlery laid before me as if I were a brain surgeon about to save a life.

That wasn't the real me—and it also wasn't the fake me anymore. I ate one meal a day solo: ostensibly to save money, but really because I didn't think I was worth feeding. I stopped seeing friends because I was afraid to spend a dime on unessential "pleasures." I would walk past bookstores where I used to waltz right in and proudly pay retail. Now I wouldn't even look in the windows, afraid to be tempted. I overdid the discipline, working fourteen hours a day trying to land assignments, jobs, anything.

And I didn't even know what work was. Should I be cold-calling strangers to get gigs? Should I be submitting proposals? What kind of work did I want? Here I was alone in my apartment. Who would find me unless I died?

I had to learn how to get out of the Lost and into the Found in terms of my career. But I also had to come to grips with the fact that I was on an emotional rollercoaster. I was thrilled to be free of office politics and meetings that I hated. But then I'd write a rent check and I'd be a mess, back at ground zero. How could I be terrified one minute and ecstatic the next?

The truth is that soloing is a dramatic turn of events. Emotions spike the way physiologists say they do for someone standing in front of a firing squad, or careening into a car wreck, or saying, "I do" before the judge. Soloing was not like stepping into another job. It was not like the first day of school. It was not like waking up next to a total stranger and wondering how you were going to get this idiot out of your bed. Soloing didn't have any quick fix.

Bubba, my pal from Houston, called. "You don't sound so good," he said. "Maybe I made a mistake," I just about wailed. "Sounds like Sadie talking," he said, meaning I was sounding like my own mother, who'd always played life safe and died just a month before, mad at the world and with just enough of a life's savings to cover her funeral. That got my gumption up. I wasn't going to end up safe. But was there a place—a perch—between safe and sound? Couldn't I be a little of both: sound, as in solid and real; and safe as in confident?

YOU'RE ON YOUR OWN

I deal with desperation this way: I don't overeat, I overwork. I begged a magazine editor for an assignment to interview Peter Drucker, the business guru, then eighty-nine, the old man of the solo sea. He liked the topic of the lone worker, and to my surprise, he agreed to the interview. Drucker is an acclaimed management expert, but he is also a soloist, a lone worker who refused for years to let his local university, Claremont College, start a business school in his honor because of his fear of becoming a person who has to take meetings. A management expert who hated groups? If anybody had advice worth following into this Unknown, it was

Peter. I convinced *Inc.* to send me out to interview Drucker, and thereby get myself some good advice.

Drucker gave me two pieces of advice: (1) It takes three years to break even financially as a solo. (2) To learn anything, you have to be prepared to teach it. He was right about the second and I proved him wrong about the first.

Doing that assignment and working on a new book proposal were temporary distractions from the fears. But the real piece of luck was to come.

George Gendron, editor of *Inc.*——a magazine for small businesses——asked me to write a series of articles about the experience of going solo, which I did for nearly a year. It was Drucker's advice, magically come to life. I learn how to solo by teaching others. I would write about what I was doing and revise my experience as I went along. I was *Inc.*'s guinea pig and my own as well. When the first diary hit the stands, no one at *Inc.* was prepared for the outpouring of letters that came in. George said he hadn't seen that much response to any story he'd published in his twenty-five-year career. People dreamed of doing the same and wanted advice from someone who'd "crossed over." One didn't just leave a company and go solo the way one left a job for another. One needs a road map to make the journey.

I learned that the word solo has two meanings: "going it alone" and being "complete in oneself." Those who go it alone outside a corporate structure often *are* alone; they are like those movie images of a lone wraith crawling on hands and knees through the desert, pleading to the vacant sky, "Water, water." They are parched for information and companionless in a world of millions of grains of sand. They have no guides and no communities. They want to have a better life by being free to work on their own, to manage no one but themselves, to find the success that is the true measure of their worth.

But you don't just leave a company/a career/a paycheck and cross over. You don't just step out of the chorus line and onto centre stage. There's more to it. There is a passage to be negotiated, a delicate transition required to go from alone-in-the-desert to complete-in-yourself. Those who dream of soloing want the courage to make the same crossing: from dependence to freedom. From the security in a job to excitement. From the fast track to a different path.

That's what this book is about: the knowledge one needs to cross over into a world where work and freedom are one and the same thing. This book is about becoming a soloist.

SOLOING AS A RELIEF FROM UNBEARABLE URGES

Why do this? It seems self-indulgent to quit a paying job because you're tired of being hassled or think you have more to offer the world. But for many, these convictions are as important as eating and breathing. Years ago I read that Steve Jobs, co-founder of Apple Computer, believed he'd die at age thirty (he's now forty-five) so he lived every day at full throttle, risking everything. Life is too short. Consultant Tracy Goss likes to say, "Someday somebody is going to come along and throw dirt on your face, so why not go all out?" Why not make your life your work rather than vice versa? Most of us aren't going to create an Apple. But we can create or recreate our own lives. You won't even know what you're missing as a corporado, but on the other side, here are the benefits that wait for you:

Soloing, *you get back your sense of identity, of being yourself*. Corporadoes cut their characters down to fit a corporate culture and lose themselves in the process. Who are you out from under those fluorescent lights? What do you really look like without that counterfeit smile plastered on your face? Who is the you who hasn't been robbed of your identity by bosses and others taking credit for work you've done? True identity is authenticity. You can only please people for so long until it starts to feel like a sickness. Then you need to go solo just to remember who you are.

Why when we are young do we think we needed organisations to get a start in life? And where did we get

Let Your Life Be Your Work

this idea that organised work could make a person feel fulfilled? The organisation is a machine, sometimes an efficient one. But to find "the force," Ben Kenobi says to Luke Skywalker in *Star Wars*:

> *Turn off your computer, turn off your machine and do it yourself, follow your own feelings, trust your feelings.*

Henry David Thoreau, America's first great soloist, had a brilliant idea for how to achieve happiness and success. He abandoned a meek civil service job on July 4, 1845 (Independence Day!) and moved— solo—to a pond he would soon make famous: Walden Pond. Thoreau gave up the idea of changing the world. "I want to be sure the world doesn't change me," he said.

That is being complete in oneself, a successful crossing-over if ever there was one. Thoreau never "fit in" around Concord, something most of us have spent a fair amount of time trying to do in organisations. We thought we could change the world, but the world tried to change us. Soloing is a means to push back, to recover our lives from corporate life, from killer schedules, from the machine that drives us.

To be sure the world didn't change him, Thoreau solo kept asking the same question of himself: Who am

I? He used so many "I's" in writing Walden that his publisher ran out of "I" characters and had to set type for the book in stages.

Remember how disparaged Jimmy Carter was as a president? When he was voted out of office, he built his own independent identity as a writer, speaker, mediator, carpenter. He's now a beloved figure, doing great work.

The second pleasure of soloing is a taste of independence. Talk shows, bookshelves, e-mails are overripe with advice on how to have a successful relationship. Business books reduce the world to management, teamwork, leadership—group behavior. But they don't describe how to stand alone—as if we are only ourselves in relation to others.

Yet independence is such a desperate and unmet need. Independence offers something no relationship can: "command and control," something we feel guilty about in an organisation, since it means inflicting control on others. But try it on yourself: It feels great when it is command and control of the self.

Psychologist Carl Jung walked out on no less a monumental figure than Sigmund Freud. If he hadn't made the break, he never would have had the need to pursue his beliefs in an alternate psychology of archetypes.

When I was growing up, I knew a window cleaner who got up at four A.M. every day. He would set out to

17

clean shop windows before the stores opened, after which he moved on to households when the families were awake. He cleaned windows so his children, when they grew up, could daydream through them. He was my dad. He didn't solo to clean windows; he cleaned windows to solo. It was terrible work, but it was freedom. "Have a boss and you're trapped. Be a boss and you're trapped," he warned me.

It took me a while to understand his lesson and live it. Now, I do what I want to do in the beautiful solitude of independent work.

The third benefit of soloing is income. The money you make as a soloist is real money. Salary money is like an allowance that your parents are handing out. It's cold hard cash. No sweat to it, no meaning to it. You never feel you are getting what you are worth in salary. You end up resenting your boss, your company, for under-paying you. Or you feel you're getting too much and are an impostor, taking money for a job that doesn't really engage you. Whichever it is, salary money seems a bit unreal. Solo money is alive. It has an emo-tional weight and personality. Maybe because it is alive, it multiplies. You can earn in one year as a soloist what it took two to earn in salary money. Will you work harder to get there faster? Will you enjoy it more? Yes.

The fourth satisfaction of soloing is illumination. Solo, I discovered that one has the chance to unlock one's deep potential. You can pursue your own beliefs. You no longer rely on Ma-Pa corporation. A soloist has no alternative but to become an adult and attain what used to be called one's "majority," the state in which a person becomes everything to himself.

Mythologist Joseph Campbell has said, "Everybody has his own possibility of rapture in the experience of life. All he has to do is recognise it and then cultivate it and get going with it. That's illumination." Heroes battle dragons on their own, solo. It's how they test themselves; it's how they know what they're made of.

That is why soloing is unlike freelancing. A twenty-eight-year-old Web designer named Matt Owens decided to pull out of his thirty-person firm and work on his own. Not to freelance but to solo. A freelancer is at the beck and call of others. Soloing is issuing the call, finding a new you rather than exploiting the old you's. As a solo, you take on new challenges. You go back to your first loves and interests. One person sheds a degree in psychology to study for the rabbinate. Another leaves investment banking to write scripts for *Ally McBeal*. You deviate from life as you know it for something less like success and more like wisdom or adventure. The differences between soloing and freelancing are these:

Soloists	Freelancers
Work to experiment on their craft	Work to pay the bills
Take on daring clients	Solicit safe clients
Risk working in fields new to them	Perfect what they alreadyknow
See work as an adventure	See work as building stature
Would rather mess up than miss out	Would rather miss out than mess up
Their ideal is being the artist	Their ideal is the professional

You see yourself anew as a soloist, and others do too. Winston Churchill was booted out of office as Britain's Chancellor of the Exchequer—a step away from the prime ministry—in 1929. He took up residence in his country home of Chartwell, writing magisterial books and articulating unpopular political ideas. But from the safe distance of soloing, Churchill was able to reposition himself. What sounded like nutty ideas while he was in office began to sound more persuasive from his country home. Churchill used his solo years to strengthen his reputation in other people's eyes. In 1940, he rose to the high office it had proved impossible to reach from within the system.

Walk out of any big organisation and who are you, stripped of that mighty identity?

Potentially bigger, better, richer than before. Why? Because you are free. Because you are free, you trust yourself more. No one is doing for you. No one is thinking for you. The result is that you become stronger, more self-aware, and more aware of big opportunities: "big" in terms of ambition, joy, and meaning.

YOU'RE NOT ALONE

It's much more crowded out there in solo land than I thought when I first left Doubleday. Who else is out there?

Gen Xers are cashing in their PEPs and TESSAs, and the knowledge they bought from their jobs in which they have all of maybe five years invested, borrowing on their credit cards, and building new businesses, mostly on the Internet, with a staff of one. *Business Week* found that of 1,000 college students surveyed, 72 per cent want to go into a business *of* their own and better yet, *on* their own. Those who start out as soloists and become entrepreneurs have a better chance of building companies in their image.

Boomers are walking out, having reached the top of their careers and asking themselves, "Is that all there is?" Remember Miles Drenttell from the 1980 baby boomer hit show *thirtysomething*? He ran the ad agency and spouted Machiavellian beliefs about competition. The real Miles Drenttell is Bill Drenttell, and just last year he sold his agency and set himself up, a lone designer working with his wife, Jessica, in an 806 area code. Wherever that is.

Sixty-somethings are going all out, determined that "retirement" will actually be an "advance." One of Rupert Murdoch's closest advisers predicts that the media baron will retire solo in the next five years. "He will hand over his business to his children, give half of his money to the rainforest, and head to a secluded compound off the coast of Australia." Murdoch's aim, this man is convinced, "is to apply all he's learned on the big stage to the small stage," where another kind of power governs and a deeper meaning applies.

One Murdoch-sized defection from the Fortune 500 will kick the trend into a stampede. When this happens, take cover if you are on the streets of a big city. It will be like a scene from Hitchcock's *The Birds*, where the skies fill with strange forms in full flight. The glass towers of corporate eyries will shake like larvae about to break open. The people inside will be ready to fly.

There'll be even more people soloing in the future because the Internet makes it so easy. It's the sledgehammer bringing down the Berlin Wall of organisations. For £120, the cost of registering a domain, you can be somebody on the Internet, even if you are somebody in bunny slippers. Even if you have a trillion bucks and you're Coca Cola, you can't put up a bigger sign. Voice mail, e-mail and mobile communications are other great equalisers between the big and the small, the scared and the confident. Pre-technology, a lone player would pick up the phone and feel he had to masquerade as his own secretary. Now everybody can sound formidable, especially if he's one of a kind.

I'll make you a bet, lonely soloist: Not only are you not alone, but Big Brother is watching you. *Inc.*'s George Gendron believes that corporations will be modeling their next work revolution on YOU. Soloists have to put stock in creativity, authenticity, commitment first in order to compete with big companies. And creativity, authenticity, and commitment are the advantage these days in a commodity economy like ours. Companies have forgotten what it means to work with artisan care. Time pressures, process orientation, emphasis on structural know-how like management and leadership are inimical to turning out great products and services.

PINK MANSION CALLING

If I had to blame one person for finally pushing me out of the nest, it wasn't some stupid boss. It was Dee Hock, a onetime big boss who is now totally anti-hierarchy.

I was still at Doubleday and editing a book by Dee, "the father of the credit card." Twenty years earlier, Dee had retired from the company he started, VISA, which he built into a world-class brand. Even as a leader, Dee was a soloist, working without peer to shape a unique and iconoclastic organisation at VISA. He left to write, paint, reflect, and recover his identity. Thoreau never had it so good. Dee built a pink mansion on the top of the tallest hill in Pescadero, California. He bought sheep and cows and a tractor he called "Thee" because he was an all-thumbs idealist like Don Quixote, and the tractor became his intractable Sancho Panza. It was "Thee and Me" for ten years, quite a solo act. Then he had to make a living again. He tore out of hibernation with the idea for a brand-new management system that combines chaos and order. He's become a one-man proselytizer for the idea, which he calls chaordic leadership.

Dee's ideas lit up my imagination. He seemed to believe there are two working "castes." One consists of the people who stay in organisations no matter what. They love to manage. The others, like me, are in organisations because we don't know any better. We think we need corporate muscle to do anything worthwhile. We are sheep, but bloody ones, butting heads against our confinement. We keep trying to break free even as we march in place.

Dee kept asking me, "How can you stand being inside a big organisation? You can't even keep a plant alive in this environment." I took his words as a sign. I looked over at the brown crumbling leaves on the window sill, and I flinched, as if the dry leaves were the symbol of my mental state. Seeing Dee's independent life had its effect on me. That pink mansion got to be a rash under my skin. It was artistry and daring that built the house, not wealth. Like the house, Dee was out in the world representing things he cared about. He started from scratch at retirement. In his VISA days, people knew his name. Now they mostly didn't know him. And few knew him as a consultant or philosopher. He was working for himself. Or, to be more accurate: He was working for the sake of delight, artistry, independence. He was urging me to do the same. "The only thing you'll ever regret about leaving the company is that you didn't do it sooner."

He was right. Dee called the other day. "How's it going?" he asked. "Do you feel like you've got your life back now?"

"Back?" I said. "This may be the first time I've had a life. For most of my working years, I was a stranger to myself. Not any more."

"You making more money now?" he asked. "You getting the assignments you want?"

"Yes, and I can't figure out why," I said. "Why should

Let Your Life Be Your Work

the simple fact of walking out of a corporation make this colossal difference in how I feel about myself and the luck that comes my way?"

"Look kid, the Buddhists got it half-right with their doctrine of reincarnation. Reincarnation exists. What they got wrong is the belief you have to die first. You can be reborn in your lifetime.

"You're getting things you want now because you're not paying attention to other people's needs; you're putting yourself first. That's why soloists find serendipity serves them better than the exercise of their will."

"Dee, how can I ever explain to anyone that soloing has anything to do with reincarnation?"

"I'm convinced that someday we'll discover there is an emotional force at work in success. It comes into play when we are free and open. Once we discover it, it will seem as commonplace as gravity. The Buddhists say, 'When one commits oneself, then providence moves too.' You can't commit yourself to an organisation the way you can commit yourself to your life. That's the difference."

In Silicon Valley, just below Dee's house in Pescadero, I was at party recently. Adam, a twenty-something who had just made millions of dollars in the sale of his company's stock, told a joke. "There was a fisherman working alone in a beautiful seaside village.

He went out every morning in the forever-blue waters and caught one spectacular fish each day. A marketing whiz happened to be vacationing in the village and said to the fisherman, 'Why catch only one fish? If you're out there anyway, why not catch a hundred, sell ninety-nine, and make a big profit?'

"'I love my life the way it is,' the fisherman said. 'Why would I want to do more?'

"'Because then you could get rich, start a fishery, move to a place like Silicon Valley, and bring in sophisticated technological systems to market all the fish. I'll be your partner and after a year or two or five of endless hours and almost never seeing the sun shine, we can take the fishery public and make millions.'

"'And what would I do with millions?' asked the fisherman.

"'You want millions,' explained the whiz kid, 'so you can take your money, buy a place in a little fishing village like this, and spend whole days doing nothing but catching one perfect fish.'"

I laughed the loudest, being the only soloist there among the corporadoes. Soloing is coming home to realise that the independence, native gifts, and ease with the self—the qualities you started out with and somehow believed you had to enlarge upon—this home is the pink mansion: the palace of the soul.

ABOUT THIS BOOK

I've learned a lot about soloing, about making the break from Ma-Pa organisation, about finding good work, about not freaking out over solo money, and about bending the world to your individual size much the way a bonsai artist makes a great oak fit in the palm of one's hand. The lessons I learned are in these pages. They range from the practical to the psychological. Often there is no difference between the two for the soloist. Inspiration determines the quality of one's work. I write about my own experience in these pages because soloing is intimate. One-person businesses hold many closely guarded secrets. Until he read my diary in *Inc.* computer designer Don Norman said he didn't know such basics as what board members are paid. By reading about my own journey, you will uncover some of these secrets. I apologise in advance for writing so much about me, but therein lie the discoveries that I hope will be useful to others.

Part One is about understanding who you are and what you want in this new life. Inventing yourself is the foundation of the soloist's business. When you know those basics, you then build your strengths into a craft. You can then bring the artist's skills to bear on your solo work. Part Two is about the business of soloing: how to find clients, build a portfolio, and deal with money issues.

I learned about the experience by talking to soloists in other fields, and by watching another solo drama unfold close to hand in the case of a man named Avram who enacted the same drama but in a different way. There are two recurring soloists in this book: him and me. Lots of journeyers go in pairs, even when the trip they take is all their own. Don Quixote and Sancho, the Lone Ranger and Tonto, Virgil and Dante, Lucy and Ricky: same trip, different postcards. I write about Avram's trip because I have seen his pains and pratfalls and achievements more clearly than I was sometimes able to observe my own. Avram is my soul mate, and as such, also my uncomplaining guinea pig.

But the day I walked out of Ze Tower, neither of us knew the passages soloing would require in crossing over. It was early July when I had just said my goodbyes to the Doubleday people I'd known for ten years. *Where was I going?* wasn't the most pressing question of the moment. That was reserved for a different question, namely: *What on earth was I thinking?*

2. Making the Break That Makes You Whole

Finally I got fired. It took a lot of work to get the company to kick me out. I had to leave first. Then they got out their stun guns.

What came first: three years of trying to leave, of telling myself it was time to go; a full year of telling Doubleday I had to go and being ignored. I did everything I could to get myself fired when I was still inside the company. Nothing worked. "You've tried to get them to let you go, and they're not reacting," said Avram. "So just retire in place." In other words, hang out. Get a tan under your office fluorescents. Wait for them to get the message.

Leaving is tough, even when you're desperate to go. "Jobs," says Peter Drucker, are "dangerous liaisons." One doesn't slip out of them easily.

It takes on average three years from the time a person decides to leave the company until the day he or she walks out the door. Those are not good or productive years. For me those were three years in limbo. Friends urged me to stay. You have the best job in publishing, they said. What will you do on your own, they said (it wasn't even a question; they took it for granted there was nothing I could do). After a lot of misery inflicted on me and others, I made the break anyway. Now I wish I had those "lost years" back. Why do people postpone this dream? What's so scary about making the break?

CRY THE BELOVED COMPANY

Gerry, who is a recruiter in the same way Colin Powell is a mere soldier, called. "Talk about breaking up with the beloved company," he said. "The other night I was having a drink with one of the Masters of the Universe. I can't tell you who, I'm sworn to secrecy. But if you came up with a list of the five big stars of corporate management, he'd be on it. He's retiring in a year. There he was like I've never seen him before, sitting with his head in his hands moaning, 'I'm determined to get out of that place when I retire. I don't want to be in my successor's hair. But what am I going to do? I don't want to run something, or be a college

31

president. Anything else would be a letdown. Who am I going to be when I'm on my own?'

"Here is a guy who is a leader of the economic free world. But he's never been a virtuoso. The thought of going solo terrifies him. It should. There are a lot of great leaders who can't lead themselves to the corner drugstore. They leave organisations at the top and disappear. Ross Johnson of RJR Nabisco. Arthur Taylor who ran CBS. They're nobody after they've said their goodbyes."

Gerry heard the musical scales in the background of my apartment. "Your piano tuner who's a virtuoso is better able to handle that world than my friend."

If Gerry's friend, CEO of a global corporation, is one step away from the trauma unit at the thought of cutting loose, who is equipped to make the break? Who gets over the wall in one piece? The head of Riker's Island, a maximum-security detention facility in New York, says the convicts who get "over the wall" have one thing in common: the desire.

So when Peter called the next day and said, "I need advice on how to leave," I said: "Just walk into your boss's office and say, 'I'm leaving.'"

"No, no," he said. "I need some *practical* advice."

A naturalist in corporate America would have a heart attack these days counting all the deer caught in the headlights. Peter is a still life. There is no more practical advice than the advice I gave Peter. But he can't hear it. He's co-dependent on his job. It's seen him through two mortgages, two marriages, three kids, a lot of goodies. He doesn't hate it. But ask him if he loves it, and he will say no. He's topped out. He's not just in a holding pattern. He's in a fast fade. People who used to say, "Isn't Peter brilliant?" now say, "If Peter is so brilliant, why doesn't he go out on his own?"

How does one get unconflicted about leaving Ma-Pa organisation? By putting it in context and knowing, emotionally and legally, what you are up against.

SIGNS THAT YOU'RE READY TO LEAVE

Every soloist says he wishes he'd left earlier. But you can only make a big break this big when you're ready. How can you tell when that is?

One reliable clue to your readiness to leave is your dreams. The unconscious is the usual site for messages that can be too threatening to pay conscious attention to.

Carl Jung, founder of the school of Jungian psychology, had been feeling uncomfortable in his role as Sigmund Freud's student and intellectual heir. As a young man in Zurich, Jung had a dream that urged him to break with Freud. In the dream, he was traveling along the mountainous Swiss-Austrian border. He ran into a peevish Customs officer who didn't seem really there, more like the ghost of an officer. "He is one of those who couldn't die properly," a bystander explains to Jung in this dream. When he woke up, Jung set about analyzing it.

The border guard stood for someone who made crossings into a new territory difficult. That was what Jung was feeling: the difficulty of crossing into a new life. The sour expression on the guard's ghostly face was much like Freud's. The dream struck the dreamer as more honest than his own waking thoughts. Freud at the time had lost much of his authority for Jung, "but he still meant to me a superior personality, upon whom I projected the father." On the one hand, he felt dependent on Freud; on the other, he resisted him. Many have the same push-pull experience with their jobs, with the corporate father.

Seeing how deeply he had internalised his despair at leaving Freud, Jung realised the need to leave was great. In a few weeks' time, Jung prepared to leave.

Like a ventriloquist, dreams can speak your fears when you can't. Elmore Leonard had been toiling as an advertising writer for many years, and writing fiction on the side. He wanted to go solo and write full-time, but was afraid of taking the risk. During this time of desire and indecision, Leonard had recurring dreams of walking down stairs, or falling, but never hitting bottom. He came to interpret the dream literally: as fear of never having a hit, that is, never having a best-seller.

Realising the dream's meaning helped him understand that he was afraid of success, and when he got over that feeling, he actually wrote a best-seller.

Then there is Geraldine Laybourne, founder of Nickelodeon, the first children's channel. Hired away to work at Disney, Gerry was struggling, never able to get sufficient wind in her sails to have an impact on that media bureaucracy. Trying as hard as she could just wore her down faster. The dream that came to her at the peak of her struggles was one in which she was drowning. She was screaming for oxygen, and woke herself up. Oxygen: She needed to get out, and breathe free. She put the pieces together for a new firm, a media company for women and children, and called it Oxygen.

Another clue to your readiness to leave is sabotage. Are you doing things to antagonize others or obstruct the system? You may be acting out what you refuse intellectually to accept: that you have already left the company, emotionally. Carolyn Myss was a medical publisher when she began to be known to a small group of people for her work as a medical intuitive: someone who can diagnose disease by intuition, particularly diseases traditional medicine cannot uncover. Myss was afraid to leave the security of her job for her unique gift. But neither could she turn her back on that gift. Myss began making promises to her publishing bosses she knew she wouldn't fulfill. Finally she was fired; she had been asking for it.

Acting subversively is like begging to be fired because you can't make the break under your own free will.

A third clue that you are ready to make the break is that you can just begin to see what lies ahead. One form of life cannot simply be abandoned unless it is exchanged for another.

Prison guards say that recidivism is highest among prisoners who have no job or family waiting for them on the outside. Begin to imagine a life on the Outside when you are still on the Inside.

I tried to do this and succeeded only partially in my plans. Still, the plans helped accelerate my leaving. I imagined having a real client. I thought about how my day would be structured: I cautiously hinted to friends that I might be leaving. But be careful. If this news becomes public, it could backfire, forcing you out sooner than you expected.

At first I was concerned when people didn't come forward with jobs and opportunities until I actually made the break. You may find this too. Don't be too concerned. The reasons people don't commit to you when you say you might be leaving is that they don't know when or if you really will be available. Once you've broken your chains, that display of bravery and self-commitment makes people more confident in working with you. Demonstrate your belief in yourself, and others follow through.

I KNOW I SAID GOODBYE BUT DO I REALLY NEED TO GO?

Leaving the organisation to go solo is like death—in yourself: you lose a big part of who you think you are. In leaving a company, you go through many stages from denial to acceptance. But it's also like leaving a marriage. In fact, going solo can be tougher than leaving a marriage—and you can find lots of advice, dozens of books, and loads of counselors on how to separate from a spouse. Since no one's studied soloists and their stress in making the break, I sought out a matrimonial lawyer, Rosaire Nottage of Chicago, to find out what people go through in order to get through. I expected her to say that leaving is tough. I didn't have a sense of just HOW tough until she described the stages of loss and separation. This is why leaving a business or real family takes years. The pain can be too great to tear yourself away at once.

"I always wonder how people ever get themselves into my office in the first place," says Nottage. Most people are in denial for a long time. This is not a leap anyone makes frivolously. "They're always looking for a justification for why they are doing this. They're always asking themselves, 'Do I have enough reason to leave? I'm not abused. Other people have a worse situation. Do I deserve to leave?'

"Things can get so bad that I ask clients: 'How come you *can't* leave?'" It's the same in the workplace, people ask if they deserve to leave the company. Why upset your life for some intangibles like freedom or meaning? How self-indulgent that sounds. But is it really? Who says you don't deserve happiness?

"It's so hard to leave because people take commitments seriously. But even more," says Nottage, "we stay because we think we're supposed to be happy in our immediate situation. We don't know what the standards are. *How happy are we allowed to be?* You don't know if the sex you're having is as good as that of the neighbor next door. You wait until you're miserable enough."

Most people don't know if their level of job satisfaction is good enough. How would you know? You can look at your salary and your perks, but these are rarely accurate measures of happiness. Friends told me I had the best job in publishing. They were right. But their opinion made it harder for me to have the confidence to leave the best job in publishing to start a different kind of life, a nonjob life. I should have heard the subliminal message in what they were saying: that if *this* job is the best, then it won't get much better. Time to get out.

STAGES OF SEPARATION

1. Making the Decision

Nottage has an ingeniously simple test for how to gauge your marriage, which could be used as a test for job satisfaction: "I ask clients to rate their marriage on a scale of one to ten. I say, 'Give me a number, right now: How do you rate it?' When a person hears himself say zero or one, that's probably the first time he heard it; it's the first time he comes out of denial. If it's a six, I say, 'What are you going to do? Throw your spouse back in and try to get a nine?'

"When someone says three or lower," Nottage continues, "I ask, 'Do you love him or her?' That creates a lot of startled looks. People often say, 'No, not really.' Ask someone who's dreamed of going solo if he loves his job, and the answer is usually, 'No, not really.'"

Like a good spouse, your job may be a steady provider. Maybe your boss is supportive, and your closest competitor is a Dilbert. But if you don't love your job any more, why stay with it?

Nottage went through a corporate divorce ten years ago. She'd made partner in a 200-person firm in Chicago. "I had achieved nirvana as a partner. But it wasn't enough. I thought my opportunities would be better on my own." She used her experience in handling divorces to test her readiness to leave her job. In less than a year, she made the break, painlessly.

2. Postponing the Decision

Like me, most people decide to leave two to three years before they walk out the door for the last time. In between they find lots of reasons to stay. Someone's

39

nice. You score a triumph. Your tests come back positive. You engage in sabotage like ignoring an important request, and nobody notices—nobody punishes you. It's one thing to leave for a great new job. It is another thing to leave when you have no "real" place to go, only some fantasy of what solo life could be.

How much energy does it take for a chick to break out of an egg? Half its body weight, at least. There's a lot of struggling going on inside that pretty porcelain-like shell.

And isn't it nice to stay? In a world where there is almost no authority in any arena, not in medicine or politics or even the family, the organisation still commands loyalty and demands obedience.

But then something happens. I got myself forced into working with one hideous client, the kind of guy who'll steal your soul and then complain *he's* been compromised. He abused my staff and then started on me—this guy who is an expert on service! He was living a lie, and I wanted no part of helping him burnish his lies. Life was just too damn short. I called my boss and said, "We have got to talk. I can do more for you on the outside." She finally heard me. The conviction had finally entered my voice.

But a declaration is not a done deal. You decide to walk, and it's like Dead Man Walking. You make the decision but it takes longer still to accept it.

3. Finishing

Call it "follow through."

"By the time people get to my office," says Nottage, "they are catatonic. They crawl up the steps to get the divorce, and they can't make it the rest of the way. They haven't pulled together the energy and resources to pull it off. They become passive and then the divorce can be a nightmare.

"They need to be able to finish. All the energy went into making the break emotionally, but that's it. They start to sabotage themselves. They disobey a court order because they forgot the date." Or in the work world, people take longer vacations and lunches, postpone decisions, and make promises they can't fulfill.

Says Nottage, "One man sat in my office and cried, 'I feel like I'm breaking up the family.' 'Duuuh,' I said. 'You are. Get real.' No one wants to be the person who breaks up the family. They just want the pain to stop." In a corporate marriage it's the same. You don't want to be at your desk, you just don't want to go through the break and the transition to another life.

4. Leave Already

Heroes are gone but not forgotten. Stuck corporadoes are forgotten but not gone. We do ourselves in by waiting for permission. It is one of the worst things about leaving a partnership like a marriage or a job.

There is a story about the legendary marketing expert Ted Levitt, editor of the *Harvard Business Review*, who wanted to resign from *HBR* to go back to teaching at Harvard. Under Levitt's direction, the magazine flourished, so his governing board was loath to let him go and kept postponing action. Levitt kept pushing. Still nothing happened. He stopped showing up for work for days at a time, thinking, "Aha! Now they'll take notice." They didn't. His bosses were willing to tolerate anything, it seemed. He finally got so desperate that he moved his furniture out of his office, and only then did his superiors realise they had to act. They reached a deal by which he was formally returned to teaching.

It's a mistake to even think we need permission.

If you've been successful, bosses feel having you around is better than the high visibility of losing you and of disrupting their own work lives. Also, they may hold onto you because they need to get accustomed to the change your leaving presents. Perhaps they really have your interests at heart. Or perhaps they are hoping you will quit outright so that the break is clean and simple and less expensive for the company.

Nottage sees the problems of asking for permission going on in divorces all the time. One spouse has a terrible time making the other understand the need to leave. "It gets so bad that sometimes they stage a breakdown.

Like jumping into bed with another person when they know the spouse is on her way home."

Just leave. Don't wait for permission. That's trying to shove the decision off on someone else. That's the passive aggressive approach, that's Bartleby the Scrivener.

But how to leave? When? On what terms? Asking for what?

IT'S THEM OR ME

If you are fired, you can go through the same emotions noted above—loss, disorientation, denial—and one other emotion: anger. But then being fired you are in a much better position to get the organisation to help you set up your new solo life.

If you think you will be fired, or are considering leaving your job to go solo, consult a lawyer. Many charge an affordable consultation fee. You'll learn about your rights, industry standards for severance, and the parameters open to you in making a break.

I hired a lawyer to represent me in my divorce, but I didn't hire a lawyer to negotiate my corporate divorce. I wish I had. Later I found out what I'd missed out on by talking to New York labor lawyer Jonathan Sack. I represented myself thinking I knew my situation better than any outsider, and I was afraid a lawyer would ruin what seemed a good deal. I just wanted to get the

43

separation signed and done. That was a mistake. Lawyer Sack—a provocative name for someone whose job it is to counsel the recently fired—takes a strong position on how solos ought to handle the break from a legal point of view.

"Never initiate the leaving," Sack advises. "The eleventh commandment is never quit a job voluntarily. By leaving on your own, you're not entitled to much. You may not get a severance. You can tell your boss, 'I think I've maxed out in terms of productivity and career growth. The next logical step is to go out on my own.' You can express your good feelings and gratitude for your years at the company. But that's starting from the high ground. If the employee opens the door, she's setting the ceiling. I prefer when the employer starts the departure process, the employer sets the floor. You can always go up from the floor."

There are exceptions. "In cases where a woman is pregnant and doesn't want to come back, it's easy to open the door to the negotiation. She wants to stay at home with the baby. Her company will offer her continued pay leave and she can start up a venture on her own."

If you must leave, ask for severance. If you have a great relationship with your boss, tell him you are thinking of leaving and hope he will say, "Okay, I'll lay you off." The benefit is that you can get severance. But bosses don't often agree to this.

You can play it cool. "Don't tell the company you're going to resign," says Sack. "Fake them out. Say to your boss, 'It's not working out. I'm not happy here because you are treating me badly (you're overworking me, you're not promoting me, you are paying my commissions late). Let's correct it, or let's discuss an amicable package.' Then you can take the package. You will have something for your startup."

Most fired employees get a standard severance package: a payment of one week to two weeks' salary per year for every year you have been at the company. Lawyers have been known to collect as much as six weeks' salary per year. The important thing about leaving is timing: If possible, don't leave before your bonus is awarded.

Leaving with a retainer has its pros and cons. If startup capital is an issue in your upcoming solo life, then consider negotiating a retainer, not a severance. A retainer makes your employer your first client. Work out a relationship with your old company to use their office space and a secretary. A retainer instead of severance allows a soloist to go out and solicit business using his employer as a calling card. "The company may prefer it too. If they have ongoing questions, they can contact you for help. Get every item in writing, because it is very easy to dispute the facts later on.

Negotiate for all the perks you can get: continuation

of health care and life insurance. Having the company continue these perks can save you as much as £6,000 a year.

Take whatever you need before you are fired or initiate severance. You're not allowed to take any property that does not belong to you. If it's the company's Rolodex, it belongs to them. If it's yours, it belongs to you.

People are often nervous about going out on their own. And scared. They take a lot of things they don't need. I took my Rolodex and used it maybe once. I found myself with a whole new world of contacts when I left.

If you feel you're being pressured to leave or are under threat of being fired, keep a paper trail. Document your protest. Write down everything. Send e-mails and memos to the person who is causing problems for you. "You have to protest," says Sack. "You have to yell, 'Stop thief.'" Such documents will help you in negotiating an advantageous departure.

What if you're not fired and don't want to be laid off? If you have put in years of great service, have the respect of your peers, you can give your company a fond goodbye. Sack contends such a person is negotiating from a position of weakness. All he has to bank on is the company's goodwill. "But the poor employee needs the company's goodwill more than company needs his." Sack said, when I told him about a friend who is resigning, "He's going to get screwed." Or is he?

NO GOOD GOODBYE GOES UNPUNISHED

The minute you say goodbye, you are no longer one of Them. If you're not with Them, you're against Them. It is difficult to leave a company on good terms, just as it's difficult to leave a marriage with the other partner in a state of total gratitude. My good friend Christopher is an expert negotiator. Even he could not leave his company on good terms, though he tried.

Christopher applied everything he knew about negotiating to leaving his company. He went to a lawyer before he resigned because he wanted information and guidance. He wanted to resign first because there was no way he'd get fired: He was a top performer. Second, he didn't want a firing following him as gossip as he began soloing. But he was also determined to ask the company to recognise him in some manner before parting ways.

He didn't need anything. He had planned his departure carefully, a year in advance. A year before leaving, he began saving money and reducing his risky investments. He found a good financial planner and worked out a way that he could live as a soloist on half his salary if he had to and still support his three children and ex-wife. When it came time to say goodbye, he hired a law firm who represented a lot of executives from his

47

company. He was going to ask for a severance.

"I wanted to know if I was at risk in offering to resign," Christopher said. "Could the company fire me? My length of service and my good standing seemed to preclude this. But theoretically a company can fire you. If you have a senior position, you can be fired at will. I didn't have an employment contract. I wanted legal help with this, and with my negotiation.

"A lawyer will give you a lot of advice that is counterintuitive. For example, my lawyer told me not to write a letter of resignation at the outset. It could potentially serve me poorly if there was a dispute. If my boss decided to fire me after I told him I was resigning, I might then be forced to say, in self-defence, that I was just thinking of resigning, and he'd misunderstood." Lawyers say there is one major reason to write a letter of resignation: if you are using it to document some entitlement you have never received, for example, if your employer has failed to pay you on time, or is withholding a bonus. Use it as a demand letter.

"My strategy was to resign at the end of the day on a Friday and give my boss time to think about it. I didn't want to come in the next day and face his angry or disappointed looks. But as soon as I rehearsed my resignation, I felt strong and wanted to do it right away.

"I began by telling my boss, 'I feel it's really time for me to leave. I want to enjoy my life.' What can he say,

'Don't enjoy your life? Stay here and be miserable with the rest of us?' I didn't want to make too much of what I'd be doing. I told him I wanted to spend time with my kids and my girlfriend. I gave him my date of departure. Then I said, 'I'm not going to take a competing job. I've done a lot for the company and I hope that the company will be generous to me in severance, and in continuing my health insurance.' Whether or not my boss agrees to that, the request will put him on the defensive. He'd have to say no, and that would make him feel he had to give on something else."

Christopher was calm about this because he'd already gone through a time of mourning. He'd been thinking about leaving for two years. "You always mourn when you leave something behind," he said. "It's like leaving your childhood behind. When kids graduate from high school, they're sad, but they're happy they don't have to repeat twelfth grade."

What did Christopher's company do? They considered his requests for the entire time of his notice until the day he left. During that miserable period he kept waiting for Daddy to descend from the CEO's office and give him some candy. He began to wish he hadn't asked for anything. "Now I'm back at the company's mercy, just as I was beginning to feel strong and free. I'm still subject to their whims." On his last day, they turned him down on every request. They even stripped

Making the Break that Makes You Whole

him of his laptop. Or tried to. In a last act of defiance, Christopher walked out carrying the computer.

I have not heard a single story of a company that didn't turn on an employee as he prepared to go solo. When you announce you're going on your own, you pose a threat to everyone you leave behind, a psychological threat, not a business threat—which is worse. Your ex-corporate colleagues act out their belief that you have demeaned them. They feel that you are saying, in effect, "I'm better than you; I can make it on my own."

RETAINER? NO!

Two years after I knew I wanted to leave, I negotiated my own retainer with Doubleday, without legal advice, and in retrospect, I too lost out. All the advantages were theirs. I thought I needed a retainer (1) to give me legitimacy in the eyes of the outside world, (2) to give me a financial stake I could count on in the coming period of uncertainty, and (3) to give me a toehold in the world I knew in case I couldn't make it in my new solo life. I was wrong on all three counts. I had more legitimacy as a solo than as a corporate player tied to a company whose reputation was mixed. And after an initial rough period financially, my earning power was strong. And I found that once I was outside the organisation, I wanted to be over and done with my old life.

Still, I didn't know any of this before I left. And after three years of hesitation about making the break from Doubleday, I was too happy with the retainer to question my deal.

Once I was free, however, the conditions of the retainer looked onerous: I had signed on to do too much work for too little pay. My health and other benefits could not be extended beyond the working agreement. The deal that got put in writing spelled out my obligations fully, but not the company's. After ten years of service and a record of significant profitability, I thought I could depend on the goodwill of the company to do right by me. As a retainer employer, that goodwill went sour. People inside the company resented my freedom; there was even less support for my projects when I was outside than when I was inside, and being outside I couldn't fight for my beliefs. Just short of my first year, Doubleday sent over a letter with no phone call or warning. The letter said they were terminating the retainer immediately. This was an abortion, a literal termination. I had no provisions in the retainer to see me through a dismissal. When I look back, I can only wonder at my stupidity.

My advice to soloists about to make the break:

1. Plan ahead. Don't expect Ma-Pa organisation to give you anything. I took two jobs in the year before I

left Doubleday. I worked sixteen hours a day: eight for Doubleday and eight on a book. It was tough. But I was determined to get cash and start building an independent identity while still on the job.

2. Leave the company without a retainer, but with a severance. A retainer ties you emotionally to the company just when you need to make a clean break to put everything you've got undistracted into your solo career.

3. Never make a dramatic change in your work life without the advice of a lawyer. A lawyer would have forced the company to negotiate earlier than they did, and would have worked out a more equitable departure.

4. Find a support system. I had Avram to complain to and other friends. They saw me over the darkest moments and helped me understand when my indecision was real and when it was phantom fear.

DEVELOPING PLAN A (AND WHY TO AVOID PLAN B)

How you make the break determines the strength and resolve you bring to your new life. One useful exercise while you are still Inside is to draw up a Plan A. This was my plan:

• List six ideal clients in three categories (clients can

be anyone to whom you provide a service or product): A (near-certain bets of getting), B (certain bets with a little work), and C (long shots).

- Under each client's name, write down three things you can do to move B and C people into the A column.

- Draft a press release announcing your leaving to send out to friends and the local press. (Even if you never go public with it, it establishes your worth to yourself.)

- Dream up three stretch goals: to speak at a major conference, to publish a paper, to learn to take photographs to use in presentations, etc.

- Build in a goal for your self-development, like learning yoga or martial arts.

- Create a solo development team: Find specialists in the areas you need help in building your new identity. (In my case these were a publicist, a speech coach, an accountant.)

- Write down the following: "This is my Plan. There shall be no Plan B. Only people who have Plan Bs need to use them."

Divorce lawyer Nottage drew up a Plan A in schedule form and followed it. "I made the decision to leave my big law firm when I was in the process of having my second child. Once he was two, I had enough energy to leave. I set a goal to leave within a year. That January and February 1987, I began to give speeches so I could network. I started learning about all the new trends in my profession. I read like crazy and asked questions. By April I was introduced to the woman who became my partner. I decided it was going to help me to stay in the mothership while I looked for the capital to set up an office. I gave my notice of leaving in August. By November, I was out and looking for space. January 1, 1988, I was up and running."

If you plan to do a lot of work with clients, you may need to add one item to your Plan A: the possibility of setting up a limited company to protect your rights. It costs as little as £20 to establish and gives you liability protection. It can also help from a tax standpoint. One hears stories like this one: A computer specialist at a major bank decided to go on his own to consult. He worked with one customer on a Y2K problem, and didn't perform the service satisfactorily. His savings, his house, all his personal assets came under risk when the client threatened a lawsuit. If a client goes after a soloist's entity, his personal assets are protected. In some cases, customers won't deal with a person who's a soloist.

Not everyone needs the protection of a limited company. A lawyer will advise you best.

A CHINESE VASE CRACKS MANY TIMES, BUT IT NEVER BREAKS

And suddenly you're free. You've pushed and tugged and finally you're reborn. You will feel bit bruised, but also stronger.

Will anything be the same once you leave? Very little. Corporate life will become only a memory. You will fall back on its lessons fewer and fewer times. You will want to phone old friends. In many cases, they will soon seem like distant acquaintances.

It's like a great Ming vase, prized all the more for the cracks that run through it. Each seam where a break has started to occur will form a scar. The scars actually make for a vase with more strength. That's how you'll be: stronger with each break.

3. What to Do with the Best of Your Life: A Test

Don't know what work you want to do when you leave the nest? How do you find out what you love enough to be joined to it at the hip?

1. What do you love enough to do it for free? Even if you think you do know, now's the time to open your mind to fresh possibilities. Job hunt manuals advise, "Be sure you find the right work." Soloists believe there is no right work. Or rather there is a lot of right work, and now is the time to try all sorts of possibilities. Solo work is a series of experiments. It is not a single path: That's what a job is. For-

get your intellectual capital for the moment. Forget your skills. Artists—which is what soloists are at heart—look for areas in which they *can't* fall back on their skills or intellectual capital so they can grow and learn.

2. What would you be happy failing at?

Cooking? Writing a piece of music? What you love enough, you'd fail at and it wouldn't be any skin off your nose. The chairman of a big computer chip company told me that when he goes solo, he wants to write murder mysteries. For a man who controls his company's billion-dollar assets down to the tenth of a penny, writing mysteries represents a bold leap into a highly speculative project.

3. How much of the financial future of your work could you live without knowing now?

When people fall in love they have no idea how the future will turn out. They don't try to know everything about their beloved. They prefer the mystery, and the discovery. That's how soloists proceed. They make outrageous, unsupported commitments of love, faith, and devotion without knowing much about the future. All you want at this point in your solo journey is to know where the heat—the passion—is for you. Where there's heat, there's light, and life.

4. This is a list of categories in which soloists typi-
cally find the work to which they commit themselves.
As you read the list, rank each possibility on a scale of
one to five, with five as the category that is most
thrilling, and one the least:

- Doing the same work I did inside the company in my
  new solo life.
    Does doing the same work hold an appeal for you?
  Of course, it won't be exactly the same. Change the
  scale, and the nature of the work changes. When you
  work under your own supervision and control, the
  experience becomes much stronger.
    Circle one: 1 2 3 4 5

- Returning to the work I did before I became a manager.
    The basic work that brought people into their pro-
  fessions in the first place inspires them to return to it
  and forego everything they hate, like doing budgets
  or reports. Most people loved designing, or editing,
  or selling, before they got promoted out of it.
    Circle one: 1 2 3 4 5

- Work I always wanted to try but was afraid I couldn't
  make a living at.
    That's me. I always wanted to be a writer/consul-
  tant, but didn't think I could take on the financial

uncertainties, so I opted for the safer role of editing/publishing.

Circle one: 1 2 3 4 5

• Realising my childhood dream.

I am always running into soloists who are talented and highly skilled investment bankers or surgeons or managers who sheepishly admit wanting to down-scale into something for which they are severely overqualified. One friend has just left the prosper-ous company she started to become a textile seller because she has loved fabrics ever since she can re-member and has dabbled in it as a hobby. A lot of en-trepreneurs tell me they thought they could realise their dream by running their own company, but then they remembered their truest dream demanded more of an intimate solo effort, a more personal commitment than even a small company could per-mit. Childhood dreams seldom go away.

Circle one: 1 2 3 4 5

• Enticed by a brand-new toy.

Phil Borges, a well-established orthodontist, dis-covered photography late in life, and fell in love with it. He left dentistry, his established profession, to try his hand at this new "toy." Five years later, it still hasn't become old to him, and he's built an international

reputation as a highly respected photographer.
Circle one: 1 2 3 4 5

5. What did you rank as having the highest priority? What had the second highest? That's the one to pay attention to. Freud said in any list where people rank their preferences, they usually put their true first choice second. What they pick first they choose because it makes them look good. Their real psychic investment is in the second-place category.

6. Describe your interest to two strangers: Write a letter to a person you admire and one you don't. Can you sound enthusiastic to each? The first will be harder than the second. You want to sound particularly good. But addressing the person you don't admire will bring to the surface the missionlike aspects of your choice, the try-and-talk-me-out-of-it position. This voice will reveal just how committed you are to your choice.

7. Now sell yourself. It took me a year to be able to look myself in the eye and say, "I am a writer/consultant with a project to sell, and not an editor/publisher." At the half-year mark, I could get out the words, but a voice that was only a whisper. Now I don't hesitate.

Solo, you'll realise, is a very intense kind of love. Or if not quite love, it is life at first sight.

4. Out of the Chorus Line and into the Spotlight

That pure light of attention is your new environment. A soloist is more like a performer than like an accountant, a deal maker, an editor. As soon as you stop worrying over whether you'll survive, you start thinking, "How can I make the most of my freedom?" The answer is: Own it, the way a singer owns the spotlight.

Frank Sinatra was a kid trapped in the big band era (like the big company era that's now passing) when he realised: "If I don't make a move out of here and try to do it on my own soon, one of those guys will do it and I'll have to fight all of them to get a position." To get a position in the spotlight, you have to show that you belong up there. The spotlight is a whole continent apart from the chorus line. It's not simply more; it's Other.

In this bizarre place of earth, attention is on you. The more intensely people watch you, the more successful a soloist you will be. Attention is your new home. You'd better get comfortable. Even if you want simply to work on your own, one needs the spotlight to get started.

FACE TO FACE WITH THE CHASTE TRUTH OF EXISTENCE

Performers have a name for the white flame of the spotlight. They call it being "up there." They say it's like the moment when you leave your body just before dying. The spotlight feels like dying sometimes. In this light, everything is magnified. One's lack of confidence is not just a shudder. The spotlight makes every hole in one's psyche look big enough to drive a Mack truck through. It does things to a performer to be "up there." Actor/singer James Naughton says, "You walk out on stage, alone and naked in the dark, and you can have a moment of anxiety. You forget your lines. It's happened to me. I looked at my fellow actor for a cue. I could see all the way to the back of his skull. There was nothing there. His eyes were like mirrors. We stood on stage for nearly a full minute of silence. I was totally alone. I could hear the stagehands say, 'He's dying out there.'" The blaze of attention on you can terrify the unwary; the fear of it can suck everything right out of your head. On the other hand, it can feel like standing in a circle of pure gold that gives you a rush like nothing else.

I wanted to find someone who could show me the difference between leaving the chorus line and owning the spotlight, literally and figuratively.

I found Linda Amiel Burns, a cabaret singer and a mentor to real performing soloists. When actor Danny Aiello wanted to learn how to handle himself "up there," to step out of an acting ensemble, he hired Burns to coach him. When *Today Show* co-host Katie Couric wanted to regain her confidence after the death of her husband, she signed up for Burns's classes. Burns teaches lawyers, doctors, executives how to take the spotlight. In effect singing is a kind of courage, and Burns's teachings can be read on two levels: how to sing, or how to use your individual traits to command attention. A great performance, says Burns, is not always about a great voice. It's about a sense of self. A passion. "Non-singers like Lauren Bacall, Carol Channing, or Rex Harrison are brilliant because they are fearless." No one but a teacher of solos can help you grasp the performance of this kind of work: what's involved in the metaphysics and manners of the spotlight. I have committed Burns's rules to memory. Sometimes they actually save me.

63

"Life is show business," Burns says. "We're always being judged on our performance and we want to rise to the occasion. We want to show that dynamic show business side of ourselves. We want not just to give a speech, but to make it work brilliantly. We're always called on to solo at something, at some time.

"Soloing offers a release from all that hiding and shrinking we've had to do for most of our lives. Soloing teaches a person to take that applause and know you deserve it. You learn to applaud yourself."

The link between singing and power is subtle but powerful. "The Japanese started karaoke," Burns says. "Soloing has caught on there because Japan is such a repressed society. People are dying for the chance to show who they are, to climb into the spotlight.

"An American came to me to learn soloing when his new client, Hitachi, had asked him to sing at one of their meetings. It was a kind of samurai moment. This is the Japanese way of seeing what kind of human being you are. They wanted to see him vulnerable and wanted to hear him sing. They knew the secret to what the music was going to do. The music was a common ground, and with that shared language of music, they could truly make each other's acquaintance. It was a test of his courage, and he passed it.

"What scares us off soloing," says Burns, "are the messages we got as kids: 'Don't be a show-off.' 'It's a bad thing to be an exhibitionist.' 'Who do you think you are?' How many people have heard that their whole lives? We're not supposed to have people stare at us and love us. We're not supposed to put ourselves on a platform. That's considered self-involvement.

"I say the opposite: 'I'm not going to hide my light under a bushel.' When people come to me to learn how to solo, they get this message: 'You have every right to be on stage.'"

I was about eighteen months into soloing when I sat in on one of Burns's workshops for people who want to come out of their professional shells and reach a higher level or more intense or more personal level of performance—and keep their fears from controlling them. To break through their own barriers, they learn to sing. And, most importantly, they learn to own the stage.

Farrah, twenty-five, a booker at a New York modelling agency who could be a model herself if she could stand the spotlight, comes to the workshop to get over her fears of standing out. She performs a song she sang as a girl to family and friends. A safe bet, but in soloing there are no safe bets. Halfway through, Farrah breaks down in tears. Brian, forty, a hedge fund manager, walks to the stage next and with an angelic smile says he chose a song that means a lot to him. He whispers out the tune. Who can believe the song means anything to him? Who can even hear it? These two would-be soloists are afraid of the sound of their own voices. Most people who step out of an organisation for the solo life are similarly afraid of their own opinions, ideas, style, and substance. One can't begin to achieve comfort with one's voice unless one owns the material: Make it your own, whether it's accounting, photography, writing, acting, investment banking. If you feel you own the material, it's yours. You feel worthy of the spotlight.

What is destroying Farrah and Brian is fear of their own strengths. The sound of their voices terrifies them. This is just a biopsy of what is going on the larger organism of their being, which is that their strengths scare them. Being seen and heard scares them. They've had so little opportunity to put their strengths to use in their working lives, always trying to blend in or to be invisible, that they don't know what to expect. They worry that by being big enough for the spotlight, they become monstrous, as if they are doing something against nature or humanity by deserving attention.

"People hear their real voices when they sing," says Burns. "The sound terrifies them because it's generally lower and more powerful than they normally allow it to be."

What separates the chorus line veteran from the person who steps forth and solos? "Soloing is about much more than singing. it's about taking a risk and not being afraid of your feelings. It's saying, 'My voice is important in the world. I can be heard.'"

Joanne gets up next to stand in the merciless white light. Joanne came to Burns's class to strut her stuff. She wants to impress everybody with how tough she is. She belts out "Hopelessly Devoted to You" with a voice that could cut through the screaming at the end of the world. It's an amazingly powerful voice, but as a soloist, she's a failure. It's not sound or spunk that wins a person the right to climb "up there." It's taking risk. Joanne is taking none. She is all technique, no heart. That serves someone in the chorus line, where power and volume are important. But in the spotlight, artistry is important. Soloing is artistry. As long as Joanne reveals no personality, nothing stamps the song as something felt, as her own song. No one can be moved listening to Joanne. She fills the stage with sound. But she doesn't own the spotlight. Linda Burns asks her to sing to one person in the class, Ivan. Joanne turns to Ivan and is silenced. "I can't remember the words," she says, though she belted them out a moment ago. Soloists make a connection to the audience; to the client. That's another necessary requirement of the art.

Joanne hides her personality behind her powerful voice just as Brian hides behind his whisper and Farrah behind her tears—just as we all hide our light under a bushel. If we hide our strengths, we cannot perform in the spotlight. Burns makes it clear that being heard is not about boldness or volume. It's about putting your full character out on display: your softness as well as your strength. That takes guts, that's a risk, and that's what a soloist is applauded for. "Joanne's hard shell which is too professional will stand in her way as a soloist," Burns says.

Great soloists make you feel you are singing to an audience of one. They don't imagine themselves simply putting out energy, one against an audience of a hundred or more. They imagine the reverse. They imagine themselves taking in energy from the hundred or more people in the audience.

A soloist convinces a person to listen by communicating a story, a feeling, something that has personal meaning for him. One doesn't solo to inform (or entertain), but to touch others. That's the difference between someone who sings and someone who sings solo.

That could not be more obvious in the last performer of the session: a mid-level Japanese executive named Rapley. He's so self-effacing, a gray man in a gray flannel suit. His fellow students are starting to pack up to go home the minute he's done. Rapley begins to sing "You're Not Alone." The fidgeting in the audience suddenly stops. Rapley's voice is nothing special, but everyone is with him. His voice is quiet, but he is singing from his heart. The song sounds so pure, a listener feels dissolved in the song. By the end, the class is on their feet applauding Rapley in tribute and to release the emotion he's stirred up in them.

BURNS'S RULES FOR SOLOISTS

Master your material so it doesn't stand in the way of your voice. I was impressed to hear that a singer has to practice and practice a song until she's ready to throw up when she hears it again. That's the point at which she's ready to go into the spotlight with it. She's made it her own. I find the parallel to soloists in other fields is that you know your task so well that you stand out in front of your expertise, not behind it. You are not a product developer, you are Don-Norman-product-developer. Your personality is what you sell. A singer has to get to that point where she isn't thinking about the words and music: The song is part of her. Then she can concentrate on feeling great comfort on the stage.

Trust spontaneity. You have to trust yourself and the magic of spontaneity. A singer learns to do setups, a brief prelude describing to the audience how the song connects to everything in his life. "People say, 'I have to write the lines down. I have to be prepared.' You don't," says Burns. "Cabaret is all about communications from the heart, whether performers talk or sing." If you trust yourself to say it right, the words will come from the heart, not just the mind; and that is where they connect.

Conquer stage fright by reducing it to physical terms. If you are panicking or fearful, soloing looks like it's Mount Everest. Says Burns: "Either climb Everest, or if that's too tough, chop the mountain down by saying, 'What does being afraid represent?' Break it down physically. How does your body react to fear? Pinpoint it. Greet your fear; say, 'Hello sweaty palms.' Make that fear your friend. Take charge. Say, 'Hello dry mouth.' Then when you've calmed your dry mouth and that's gone, the shaky foot will start. You need to feel you can do no wrong on the stage."

Watch what your body is saying. "Soloists sabotage themselves with terrible body language, like cringing. The message is, 'I won't take up too much of your time.' Or hunched shoulders. Be careful how you use your body. It gives away all the fears of soloing."

Love the applause. Burns coaches beginners to see the spotlight as a circle of golden light, as if she were Virgil trying to get Dante released from hell and accepted into heaven. "This is what the magic is when singers are up on stage. They think, 'This has been so wonderful. Why did I think it was as terrifying as Everest. This feels good.' We're all so guilty about feeling good; we think something bad is about to happen.

"Love the feeling; make it last. Pain lasts long enough. Train yourself to make the pleasure last by putting yourself in that golden place as often as possible.

Soloists learn to love the applause. I see beginning singers who when the applause comes, turn away or talk through it. It embarrasses them. They're not supposed to want it. I tell them to drink it in. I give them permission to enjoy it. That's how they learn how to make it last.

"Last August I got a call that my son was in a coma after a car accident. I had to finish a show that night. I couldn't face the fact that my son would die or be crippled. I didn't say anything to the audience. I got up on that stage, and it was healing for me too. It's such a magical place, nothing can hurt me there. I did the performance and got on a plane to be with my son. When I got to the hospital, he woke up.

"In soloing *people create a world that is not in their world*, a world of friendship and love and music. Those parallel worlds are essential for living in the 'real' world. They preserve you, they spare you."

Don't run away from your demons. Soloing is an immediate assignment in growing up. You can't take the stage convincingly if you're a mess. Says Burns, "Sometimes I assign songs to people. If they're hiding their sexuality, I give them a sexy song. I assigned one girl an angry song. She said, 'Why are you giving this to me?' They think when they sing an angry song, the anger won't stop. If you hide the anger, try to force it down, it will come out in destructive ways."

71

That's what it takes, guts-wise, to step out from the crowd, let your talent shine, and not back down from fear of being noticed. The transition from chorus line to spotlight is not something you go through once. You go through it every day. That's if you're lucky. Otherwise you go through it every hour.

5. Brand-New You

Six months after leaving the corporation, I found myself drifting further and further from safe shores. I could see clients on the distant horizon. I could shout to them, but nobody was paying attention to me. Who was I and what did I have to offer? Issues of identity are major hurdles in the solo life. A period of introspection is vital after leaving the corporation. In a way, soloing forces you to grow up. You realise you can't count on Ma-Pa corporation any more. Time to hurry into maturity. Time at last to ask, "Who am I?" Because that's what clients will see.

When people look at you, who or what do they see? And can you shape their perceptions, just as any great brand shapes the perceptions of the market?

Most brands are product-specific. Disney is Mickey Mouse. Nike is the swoosh on sportswear. Some of the most powerful brands today, though, are essentially solo brands. Martha Stewart. Calvin Klein. Steve Jobs, who is Apple. Bill Gates, who is Microsoft. What do great brands have in common? A promise.

To create a brand of yourself that draws clients and work toward you, what do you do? You figure out what kind of promise you want to make to the world.

As the publisher of Currency Books, I created and managed a brand: a promise to deliver quality ideas packaged in books that looked as good as the best non-fiction published. Alone, I wasn't sure what my new promise would be. I engaged in a period of introspection and research into what brands are.

Branding is not a mechanical exercise. What follows will take you into the reaches of your psyche and sense of self.

A LOOK IN THE MIRROR

You may think you know yourself and therefore also your brand, but your perception may be totally different from the reality. No one can make a promise when he is distrusted by others, and if you trigger perceptions in others that are totally different from the reality of who you are, you need to do something about the discontinuity.

I came to grips with this when I asked consultant Fernando Flores to offer his assessment of me. I saw myself as a source of insight into the trends shaping business, more powerfully now than when I was at Doubleday. Fernando put the kibosh on that self-perception. He said, "You remind me of a Buddhist monk who has turned her back on the world and is waiting to die." My hard-won freedom, my escape from the corporation, he saw as an abdication of effort and responsibility. The promises I was making—to deliver an article here, a speech there—seemed to him too small. "You played a role in the world of power," Fernando told me, "a world of big publishing, but it disappointed you and now you've given up on it. You must come back to it. You must find a way to use what you know about power."

He was right. When I heard that, I began to reassess the jobs I was taking, and to present myself differently to clients and others. I began to ratchet up the stakes.

Every soloist needs to gather assessments to understand where her promises to others fall short of her self-perception, but also where she might be stronger than she suspects. You can't do assessments totally by yourself. You need to engage in a dialogue.

"There are two tennis games in any tennis game," says consultant Tracy Goss. "The people in the stands see a game of great skills. If you're on the court, there isn't something called 'great skills' going on. Skills are only appreciated from an observer giving an account."

You need a community you respect that may have an assessment of you. You cannot do it mechanically. You need to cultivate trusting relationships.

Why? Where are we heading? Toward the secret life of brands.

WHAT IS A BRAND?

What qualifies as a brand? Flores defines a brand as a promise, a commitment. Federal Express is a promise: to have your package delivered by a certain time on a certain day. The post office is a prediction. It estimates your letter will arrive someday in the future. That's why FedEx is a brand and the postal service is a fuzzy concept.

You have to make lots of promises to people now that you are out on your own. The more promises you make and fulfill, the stronger your brand becomes. As a publisher, I promised to inspire people to write the best book they could. I delivered on that promise consistently. Now that I'm solo, I promise to guide people to brave new worlds of creativity. I do this throughout my activities as a writer, consultant, adviser. Every commitment I take on has to reinforce that promise, to guide people to new worlds.

I came to this conclusion in thinking about the one consistent thing I did throughout my career. One thing soloing does is force you to get to know who you are. No other work makes that so imperative. *You have to know yourself to know your brand.*

You are the commitments you make and the promises you keep.

Be careful what you promise. That's how you become known.

Promises and commitments are how we build our identity. We make promises to people every day: We loan them a book, or deliver a project, or help with contacts.

That is also how we can begin to change negative assessments of ourselves. There is a mirror effect to our promises: how others get to know us determines how we see ourselves. It's like school: If your teacher believed you could do advanced maths, you rose to the occasion. If she considered you a flake, you came to see yourself that way. Martha Stewart, another great American solo brand, is known for the quality of Martha-ness: upper-class chic sold at mass-market prices. Martha is known by the promises she keeps.

DEEP DOWN

Brand literally means "a burning piece of wood, a mark made by a fire, a sword," according to the *Oxford*

English Dictionary which dates the word's first appearance to Chaucer, the poet of the Middle Ages. Brand-new means "new from the fire," fresh and bright, with all the excess burned off. Swords were tempered in the fire until every ounce that wasn't tough was evaporated. Strong brandy is burnt wine, distilled wine. That process holds a clue to what brands are: Burn or distill a substance and you burn off all that is unnecessary and trivial. What you are left with is the essence, the strongest version of an otherwise pale or ordinary substance.

A brand is your essence: who you are when you burn away all that is excess. Dr. Seuss wrote a poem on the art of eating pastries: "Bite down on what's real," he says, "and spit out what's air." The greatest solo brands of the second half of this century—Nelson Mandela, Vaclav Havel, Martin Luther King, Gandhi—were tempered in prison, in the fire, as it were. There, one loses everything but what is essential in one's character. Heroes in myth are always tested in the fire of some extreme challenge. They come out standing for something: Mandela stands for humanity; Havel for the power of the powerless; King for moral courage; Gandhi for non-violent change.

What's left of you when you spit out the air, in Dr. Seuss's terms? Or your airs in social terms? How do you burn down to the essence of your personality?

INVENT NOTHING, DENY NOTHING

This is the key by which a soloist finds his brand. *Invent nothing* means to add no airs or embellishments to your character. Encourage no extra assumptions about who you are.

Deny nothing means make use of all your strongest and best traits, particularly those you had to hide to fit into corporate life, even perhaps a trait that has embarrassed you in the past. The characteristic that embarrasses us most can also be the source of our greatest energy and creativity. Like strong opinions. Or unique approaches.

As mentioned, Carolyn Myss denied her gifts of diagnosing illnesses that defied doctors' comprehension. Even when a professor at Harvard Medical School decided to collaborate with her, she went on hiding these unique skills while employed in her day job as a medical publisher. Finally, the division of labor caught her bosses' ire. She was fired. Solo, she forced herself into recognizing her unique brand.

Who would we be if we invented nothing and denied nothing? Lots of people have fantasy jobs that they spend most of their lives denying. It's not that they deny all fantasy. Often people build up the wrong fantasy: They pretend they are born marketers or the baddest VP that ever walked the corporate plains. Why cling to a false fantasy, when your own deep-seated fantasy is so much truer, and potentially the source of life-sustaining work?

The habit in Carpet Land, or most corporate headquarters, is to embellish everything and reveal nothing. That's because no brand is meant to compete with the company brand.

BUILD CHARACTER, NOT EGO

I worried whether the whole idea of branding was an invitation to one's inner egomaniac. Was soloing too self-centred? But then I thought: Does Coca-Cola worry about coming on too strong or being too noticeable? What's Coke but sugar water? Why then would I, who could be of service, feel shy about reinventing myself as a brand? Kids learn not to be afraid of their own shadow. Why should adults be afraid of their own light?

Carl Jung said that people are more frightened of their strengths than they are of their weaknesses. If we knew how good we are, Jung believed, we'd have to act on our potential. Many talented people end up accomplishing a shadow of their abilities.

Soloing requires acknowledging how good you are. This is especially tough after being in a corporate environment. Every corporate being experiences this tremendous nakedness on stepping out of the corporation: Companies serve "as an armour in which the tender self could sally forth into battle with the world," writes historian Leo Braudy. One of the safety valves about a company is that it detaches a person "from the more debilitating aspects of individuality."

Individuality is tough. When it's you and nothing but you on the line for your success—when you can't blame anybody else—if there's a failure, it's your failure, it's your fault. If someone says no to you, they're rejecting you. The dark side of "you are the brand" is that there is no place to hide.

Making promises, which is the work of building a brand, actually keeps you honest, because it forces you out of imagination and into action. You become known by the promises you make.

Before you can make legitimate promises, you must learn to listen to assessments of you. This is an important first step, because you must learn where the promises you make now are inspiring trust and commitments in others. You need to know when you are being honest about your own promises, and when you are bullshitting others. We lie to ourselves more than to anyone else. Assessments root this out.

Appreciate what brands mean and one needn't be shy of their effectiveness and power, let's take this art of assessments a step further, in a formula devised by Flores.

Ask your closest friends or colleagues to assess your strengths and weaknesses. Tell them that they can say anything they want and the only response you will make is, "Thank you very much. I appreciate your sincerity."

Ask them to give you three opinions of you: Where do they feel you fall short of being the person you think you are? What do you do that is not worthy? Ask them to end by stating a positive opinion of you. What do you do well, maybe better than anybody else they know? Ask them to make their answers as specific and rich in examples as possible.

Why get the bad news first? Because you'll listen harder. If you hear the good news first, the negative assessment will lose its sharpness. And if a friend is asked to deliver the good news first, it could make her hold back on the negative assessment.

Besides, strong players like tough criticism. It makes them stronger.

You might get an opinion like: "My assessment of you is that you start a lot of projects but never bring anything to completion. You get excited at the start and then you fade away, which leaves me disappointed. Your promises don't inspire trust."

Be prepared to hear that your image of yourself doesn't totally correspond to how people see you. A young, highly successful CEO heard that his ambitions outstripped his self-confidence, and that without the latter he would never achieve his goals. Tough stuff, but vital. We all live with big inconsistencies in our lives.

They get in the way of making promises we can keep, promises we have to keep if we are to define our identity and our brand. We need to know how we are seen by others. If the message comes back to us that we cannot be trusted to do what we say, we must take this into account. Either we are overpromising or we're denying the truth about ourselves.

MAKING THE BEST PROMISE YOU CAN MAKE

A soloist creates a strong brand by creating a lot of promises and commitments, but also by making a certain kind of promise.

Here is the essence of building the solo brand:

The more promises you make, the stronger your brand becomes.

If you are not making promises that are bigger than you think you can keep, you are going to be bored.

What promise do you want to make to the world? An *Inc.* reader named Mike wrote me:

I have been a soloist for ten years. I write articles for food and beverage trade magazines and do marketing communications consulting when I can find the work.

I still can't figure out who I am and like many
soloists, my biggest difficulty is marketing myself. Last
year, I had, for me, a terrific year. This year has
started out terribly slow, and while I've networked
and wracked my brain to come up with ideas to gen-
erate new business, I'm stumped.

He is right to link these two conditions: Know yourself—your identity—and you have a promise to market. Let's deconstruct Mike. Why, having paid his dues,
is it so hard for him to come to terms with who he is
and what he's about? Why can't he figure out who he is
and shape an identity he can market? Who is he under
all that insecurity?

Mike has two children. He dreamed of being a
writer and wrote two mysteries, which he had published, but never made a penny out of it. He needs to
earn money to support his family. He still has dreams
that won't let go of him. But they fall short of turning
into a promise. The reason is in his language:

I love food. I know a little about it. I like writing. I
seem to be pretty good at it. So I play with ideas that
utilise one or both skill sets (I don't seem to have any
others). I have prototypes for a dried pasta side dish in
a niche no one's in, but I don't have the business acu-
men (or resources) to manufacture and sell it myself. I

have business plans for two terrific restaurant concepts that, again, I don't have the business sense to pull off myself. For fun, I've started writing a children's book for my daughter since no publisher wants the mystery series I was writing. But I don't know where to truly put my energy. It's a little frustrating.

You can hear the defeat in his words: Every line of hope is followed by a line of resignation. All his hope is co-dependent on certainty of failure in his mind. Why? Because Mike is not making promises that are bigger than he can keep. In fact, he is not promising anything.

Mike is stuck in a dangerous belief system. It's the belief system that's guaranteed his success up to now: survival in the face of his dreams. The message in his self-analysis above is: "I have to minimise my dreams because I have no practical sense or acumen." That is how he keeps a rein on himself. And that is precisely what a soloist cannot afford to do.

A soloist makes promises and then lives up to the promises.

How does someone like Mike get out of his trap?

QUIT THE SURVIVAL MENTALITY

You have to get past your survival mechanism to know what is essential to you. The first step is Getting

Out of Your Own Rut. Kiss it goodbye. Survival, your instinct for it, has made you effective, but not a success *to yourself*.

Survival is whatever job you're good at doing: your thing. *Mike's survival is wrapped up in not being able to do something, but trying anyway.* The jobs we have held for a long time compensated for our insecurities. Look back at Mike's language: It's the language of survival, not success. He seems more invested in the reasons that his dreams and passions cannot succeed than in the reasons that they could.

My friend Darcy takes on lots of little projects, things that don't really challenge her to take a dangerous step which, with her personal charisma and brilliance, would be a walkover. She flirts with meaningful projects but abandons them halfway through. She manages not to be around when the "grade" comes in, and people working with her were for a time saying, if only Darcy had stayed on, this would have been a great project. Now her gambit is creating distrust in others, dismay over promises unfulfilled.

To get beyond the survival frame of reference, you have to consider questions you may never have asked yourself because they served no purpose, until now. You have to put your success at risk, as Tracy Goss likes to say. Answer the following questions for yourself. They will boil you down to your essence:

1. What thrills me?

2. What makes me different?

3. What's my most noteworthy personal trait?

4. How would the person who respects me most characterise me?
- as a number one problem solver?
- as a creative genius?
- as an organiser par excellence?

Mike needs to think of himself in these terms if he is to discover his brand. So does any soloist in search of his brand.

A soloist has to give up the fears that have kept him stuck to a small game and a small identity. He has to concentrate on what thrills him, and not on the reasons that he thinks his dreams will never come to pass. How does he know? Why fear failure before there is any palpable need to fear it?

I asked myself: "What is it about me that people most enjoy?" Not what do they enjoy about my work, or about the articles I write, *but about being in my presence*? In Mike's case, why did magazine X choose to work with him? Is it that he has ideas that would inspire them? That he might challenge their audience in ways they had never been challenged?

LOOK AT WHAT'S MISSING

Now think about what's missing from your life:

If you could do anything, if making a living wasn't necessary, what would you do? (Stop thinking about doing something to survive. That keeps you small and handcuffed. *You can't play a game for success and for survival at the same time.* Each draws on different skills and a different mindset.)What's missing in your life? Asking yourself this is how you get to an understanding of what's possible for you. What's your goal? Money? Fame? Love? Adventure? And the big question: *What is important to me?*

There is power in being specific in your answers. Not: "What's missing in my life is joy." But: "What's missing in my life is the chance to be heard, and recognised, for my ideas." Or: "What's missing in my life is real contact with people as their financial adviser and life planner, or mate, relationships where I can touch others' souls."

The more specific you are, the more clearly you begin to see what you can promise because you passionately want to deliver on that commitment.

CAN YOU IMAGINE A FUTURE WITHOUT YOU?

Imagine that your great-grandchild has just come across your papers in an antique store or the dustbin of a library. What will she think?

What is your legacy? What are you remembered for? And what do you want to be remembered for?

Woody Allen said, "I'd like to live on in history, but I'd much rather just live on in my apartment."

Death is thought by some to be the most beautiful gift mankind is given, because it sets us free. Tracy Goss says, "Somebody's going to come along and throw dirt on your face anyway. Why not pull out all the stops and do what you've always dreamed of doing, even if you fall flat on your face. So what?"

IF YOU CAN ACCOMPLISH IT, IT'S TOO SMALL

What goal would you accomplish if only you could?

Declaring a big dream—one you can't accomplish in this year or next—is the promise you make to yourself.

I want to write a novel on the life of a historical figure. I'm not doing that today. I'm not acting on that wish or planning how I can do that right now. But knowing the promise shapes everything I do as a soloist, indirectly but powerfully. A soloist who makes a big promise to himself finds he meets people who, when he tells them his big dream, may know something about it or can help him in some way. Because I often mention what this dream is, it becomes a part of me, like my curly hair, which I also don't think about but which also gives me a certain image in the eyes of strangers.

THE STORY OF YOUR LIFE

By thinking through these issues, you burn off a little more of the unnecessary fat known as fear and embellishment and you zero in on who you are and what you want to be known for: the essential matter of building a brand.

A brand is a promise, and often it gets expressed as a revealing story. FedEx is the story of a former airline pilot, Fred Smith, who twenty years ago wondered why packages couldn't be treated with the same care as passengers. That in a nutshell is Smith's story. Steve Jobs's story? Perpetual outsider, orphan, troublemaker establishes Apple—a brand of computer "for the rest of us." Phil Knight's story? So-so athlete teams up with the greatest running coach Bill Bowerman to make waffle-iron running shoes—Nikes—that gives ordinary runners the same tools as professional athletes. In the case of each of these companies, a personal story—a solo story—was so powerful that a company was born. Brands are often born in stories.

At the heart of stories is a personal anomaly, a mismatch between you and the given world. Knight, the poor athlete, promises a shoe that guarantees great performance. Jobs, the maverick orphan, promises a computer that gives PC orphans an identity. Then of course there is Martha Stewart, the lower class girl with upper-middle-class tastes reworks the concept of the highbrow to mid-level affordability.

The most moving story of a brand built on an anomaly is this one, told by Fernando Flores.

A mother lost her daughter in a drink driving accident some fifteen years ago. Her friends tried to comfort her by saying it was an "accident" and she could not hold herself responsible. She knew her daughter's death was *not* an accident, and she *did* hold herself responsible. That was the anomaly. And that became the basis of the story she told herself: that she could do something to show the world that "accidents" were not accidents at all; that they could be prevented. She created a system whereby kids at a party where alcohol is served would nominate a designated driver, in order to transport them safely. She branded her anomaly, her idea, her story, in the organisation called MADD, Mothers Against Drunk Driving, one of the most successful branding stories of the last two decades.

What's your story? What links your biography to the promise made in your brand?

To understand my own story, I did a simple exercise: I took my résumé and rewrote it as a marketing sales brochure where the product/service is me.

The way I used the ten questions above to dig deep into my promise and story is this: I studied what persisted in my career, no matter where my various moves led me. I needed to discover that essence, and the question helped me focus in on the patterns of my past.

Consistently, what thrills me is being a journeyer, a guide. Business thinkers have been known to follow me in my wanderings, looking with interest at what interests me. I take people to intellectual destinations that change their lives. That is the start of my story line.

Rewrite your résumé this way, and you will have the basic plot of your story.

When a soloist's story works, it is very simple and has a subliminal impact: a feeling beyond and deeper than the feeling expressed in words. It is all the more powerful for working just slightly below the level of consciousness. John F. Kennedy identified himself with Camelot when he rose to the presidency, the most solo role in the political system. A white knight carries a lot of positive sentiment as a symbol. Today people look at JFK's dark side, but it is never so dark as it might otherwise be because of the identification with Camelot.

"I ALWAYS KNEW SHE'D GET INTO TROUBLE"

For help with your story, go back into your far-flung past. Whom did your teachers say you would turn into? Were you always a troublemaker? Is there some stand-out event in your life that led you to take up the work you want to do solo? Think about what you have chosen to do in terms of history—your own and your family's history. Perhaps, as is the case with Fred Smith, Steve

Jobs, Phil Knight, and Martha Stewart, your history plays a direct role in the work you are born to do: in the essence of your branding.

Ford has a history, which gives it an identity. Apple, Intel, Microsoft; every major company has a sharp identity. A soloist needs to mine her own history just as much.

Do not feel trapped by the facts of your history, that you were born to bad parents and so have no history to mine. Your history is not some set of sacred facts. History is an interpretation, and your history is yours to interpret. To know the history and then reinterpret it gives you additional depth.

Fernando Flores said to me, "You have arrived at a point in life where you want to invent yourself again, tired with playing the power game which had come to seem empty and a source of disappointment." His advice: "Consider yourself as something *invented by you*. Consider the fact that you are the story you tell about yourself."

Flores had a frightful history. He was imprisoned for three years for political democratic aims in Chile. When he tells his audiences about this experience, the respect they show him is devotional. He describes being confined to a concrete cell, often held in solitary confinement. He would hear gunfire, not knowing whether his captors were killing his friends who were also imprisoned, or if they were tricking the prisoners into believing the next round of fire would be aimed at them. His story awes listeners. His history becomes his promise and his brand; a consultant who teaches companies how to achieve freedom and new possibilities for themselves out of circumstances that seem all-constraining, even imprisoning.

Flores decided to reinvent himself and his history when he won his release. "I could have come out of prison as a victim of Pinochet, describing the torture to anyone who would listen, angry, out to settle a score. *But I told a different story about my history, and that story shaped my identity and my business.* I say that prison taught me about freedom, not confinement. I say that Pinochet taught me about freedom, and how one sets oneself free by the power of words. I have become a symbol—a clearing—for others to enact their own freedom, to get out of the bullshit that's holding them back.

"To reinvent yourself," says Flores, "understand that the invention called you is something co-created in a historical context.

"You and your story don't just rise out of the ashes. They come from somewhere." Fate dealt Fernando a prison sentence. But the story he tells—his interpretation of it—is his own reinvention. The promises he makes—to teach the behaviour of freedom—derive from this story. His history makes him and his brand larger than life.

Introspection over. But there is one more step in making yourself a force that is a brand. That step means paying attention to the surface, or as advertising maverick Jay Chiat once put it, in this culture everyone has to learn to be "deeply superficial." The joke is spot-on. You are your promises, and reinforcing that is what people see.

Sculpture

6. Bend the World to Fit the Palm of Your Hand

What can one person accomplish alone that is satisfying? This is an important question, because when you go solo, you don't necessarily downsize your ambitions. Many soloists want to have more influence, not less, and the focus afforded by soloing makes that possible. Maybe you are not looking for the next big job, or the next major accomplishment, but to achieve joy or peacefulness. That is also a pretty big aim. For many, the aim is to be even more effective than with a corporation behind you—but on your own terms.

One doesn't need a large span of control to accomplish anything significant. Proof: Frank Sinatra, a sole figure out on stage in the spotlight.

Proof: Some of the greatest painters of the twentieth century worked on miniature scale. Proof: The laws of nature and esthetics that created a new economy built on the transistor, then later on the even smaller microprocessor, and before that on the arts of bonsai and the Japanese lunch box. The world is getting smaller: It's reaching a size that's perfect for the soloist. Work is being redefined as intimate and personal.

So what does a soloist do to attain influence? Leverage the strengths of being a single person in a complex world. Companies can do some things by sheer muscle, but they can't do others.

Here's what you trade in when you go solo, and here's what you gain:

- A soloist gives up Resources for Chaos. An employee has budgets, minions, and a small amount of fuck-up room. A soloist has no budget, no minions, and a lot of fuck-up room. You can flourish with no money but lots of room by taking on experimental projects, by promising clients depth of experience, and by working in arenas where business is changing every day, particularly in the information economies.
- A soloist renounces Scale for Intimacy. You can't design big projects. But you can design big ideas. And you can approach the impact of scale by creating

communities beholden to you. Put people in touch with one another, as Don Norman does by means of his Palm Pilot organiser containing 10,000 names, and you start communities built by your own design.

- A soloist sacrifices Power for Freedom. Everybody who's worked for a living understands power, but when it comes to freedom, we're babes in the woods. It's scary when you don't have anyone telling you what to do. Sartre called freedom "nausea." Soloists need to know how far they can go without tempting the forces of destruction. Sometimes this means choosing fewer assignments and delving deeply into them.

- A soloist forgoes Control for Self-Destiny. You are in charge of no one but yourself: not by becoming your own worst boss, demanding and never satisfied. As your own boss, you should choose only what you love to do with the people you love, so you don't squander your talents but rather see them grow.

- A soloist trades the Comfort of Routine for the Intensity of Projects. One of the main reasons people consider giving up soloing is that they love the downtime of a job: long lunches, gossip, breaks, interruptions. But when you see how much influence you can have as a solo, the intensity starts sucking you in.

- A soloist forgoes the benefit of teamwork and lots of opinions for the ability to turn on a penny. Even the fastest organisations can't operate with the speed of one person.

Control of the self. Freedom to experiment. Intimacy. Speed. And depth. Leveraging these qualities is the key. Resources, scale, power, and comfort come to seem like encumbrances, because in the solo world, they often are.

"The principles of control and discipline ought to be abandoned in favor of self-control and self-discipline," wrote Vaclav Havel, president of the Czech Republic, who rose to that position after years of soloing, as a poet of the revolution, then as a prisoner in solitary confinement. Havel wrote a manual on freedom and effectiveness, called *The Power of the Powerless*. In it, he asked how it is possible that huge regimes would topple when a lone poet wrote or a singer sang. The reason has a lot to do with the power of the sincere and authentic voice. One voice can have huge impact.

A poet points out that the emperor is naked, Havel remarked; and sooner or later, the big power has to confront this criticism, either by silence or with a response.

Confront big institutions with self-control and self-discipline. Convince yourself first that as one person you are not small but singular. Retrain your senses. Understand that one voice can be more powerful than a chorus.

For a time, what I'd given up in going solo dominated my thoughts. The paycheck. The systems. The administrative help. All of that vanished when I left my job. At one point, two corporate refugees, David and I, were talking about all the things we could do as newly minted Jean Valjeans who'd been lucky enough to be set free. I said I would study the theatre of leadership and put on performances in lieu of boring old speeches. David was going to create a tape series so he could sell his advice and not have to travel everywhere in person. Suddenly we looked at each other in terror. I was late for the post office, where I had to mail out the day's bills. David had a supper meeting where he'd be primping for some advantage in landing a client against the competition, McKinsey and Company, one of the largest and most prestigious consulting firms. Here we were, two solos with big dreams and not a lot of money to invest in them. I couldn't and wouldn't get a secretary. David couldn't take the time from rushing after clients to make it possible for him to stop rushing after clients. Who were we kidding? What kind of influence could two small potatoes like us hope ever to have?

Every kind, Havel would say.

BETTER AT SUBTRACTION THAN ADDITION

The solo state of mind requires nothing more than a different kind of maths. Stop adding things up.

Soloing reduces you to the essence. The process is more like how one becomes a poet. One is reduced to it. Kay Ryan, a writer in San Francisco, says, "Instead of being the result of refinement and purification of the blood until only poetic ichor runs, the poet may be the product of some cataclysmic simplification, much like the simplification that overtook the dinosaurs, wiping them out and leaving the cockroaches. Both cockroach and poet are hardy little survivors, quick and omnivorous." Ditto the soloist.

You have to adjust your vision when you solo. If *you* see the possibilities in a contained world, so will others. You have to see them differently to be able to sell them with confidence.

Artists see how a small thing actually contains the wide world: Surrealist Marcel Duchamp said, "The botanist's magnifying glass is youth recaptured. It gives him the enlarging gaze of a child . . ." Thus the minuscule, a narrow gate, opens up an entire world. The detail of a thing can be the sign of a new world which, like all worlds, contains the attributes of greatness. Miniature is one of the refuges of greatness.

Duchamp measured for infinitesimal qualities, while his friend, artist Joseph Cornell, tried to capture the ineffable with the utmost precision and delicacy. Cornell tended to work poetically. His artworks were small, imaginary theatres. He assembled pictures or dramas in boxed assemblages: a stuffed parakeet, a cash register, a doll. He and Duchamp not only changed the way art is made; they changed the way it is perceived.

"For Cornell," art historian Walter Hopps writes, "even small experiences could be virtually overwhelming. He would fill a pillbox with pink sand, then stare at it as if it contained a whole universe of events." Cornell was once spotted alone at a department store bakery, examining a slice of angel food cake with a magnifying glass, "as if he were exploring the surface of the moon. Cornell had a great interest in tiny phenomena."

Readjust your sight, and everything that was small appears infinitely large. Gianni Agnelli, founder of Fiat, was once asked to explain the secret of his success. He said that every morning he would take coffee on his balcony. He would allow his gaze to drift out over the water as far as it would go. Then he would reel it back in to focus on the items on his daily agenda. He would repeat this process several times. Throughout the day, he would bring the memory of that big horizon into seeing the matters close at hand. The habit of seeing things close up from a distance gave him the patience to deal with small matters in a big way.

THE JAPANESE LUNCH BOX MODEL

There are parallels to the soloist's ideal world in the humble and tiny Japanese lunch box.

Kenji Ekuan, Japan's foremost industrial designer, tells of inviting a guest to his home. They talked for hours until it was time for dinner, and by then only a "make-do sort of cold meal easy to order from a nearby restaurant" could be found. "Fearing the little sectional-ised wooden container might seem too plain and simple to my guest, I placed a single blossom on its lid as a decoration."

Ekuan's guest lifted the blossom and opened the tiny box. "He exclaimed in surprise at the universe of color and variety hidden inside the diminutive square lac-quered box. 'Beautiful,' he said. He told me that he could clearly sense the reduction of the many to the one in the concept of the lunch box."

That's the way it is for the soloist. You reorient your-self from the many to the one, and because you appreci-ate this act of magic—the powers of the many in less—others see it too.

How do lunch box artists turn the small into the large? Not by genius, they say, but by the lunch box. "The lunch box itself supplies the genius," says Ekuan. "A myriad of desires may indeed be set in a well defined one-foot-square enclosure; and, having put in every-thing you can, the box is filled with a sense of tension." With every assignment a soloist takes on, he is building a Japanese lunch box. In a solo world, the focus is on the one issue, problem, story, the idea close to hand, the intimate, personal touch: All these stand for more because they are so unusual in a mass-produced, overly professionalised world. There is nothing dull about the ingredients found inside a Japanese lunch box. Everything is included, so nothing loses force. In this context, "all ordinary things become extraordinary."

Aesthetics, voice, personal imprint: those elements matter. Corporations extol service, but for them service makes a transition "seamless" and invisible. Solos, by contrast, want the transaction to be noticed; the contact, and everything that is part of it, should be rich, meaningful, worth stopping and remarking on. If it's worth a minute of the client's time, it's worth making the experience beautiful. Tibor Kalman, the designer, would send a one-of-a-kind gift to his clients, usually on some obscure holiday that no one else was celebrating. One year he sent out an old book, each volume different, with a new twenty-dollar bill as a bookmark, and a suggestion that the client match it and donate the money to charity. Any small, surprising gesture of a soloist can have a big impact.

Probably the most important element of the lunch box is that it satisfies hunger. The lunch box's astonishment is that it draws on what is near to hand but always emphasizes variety. The soloist too must emphasise the variety in her experience as well as the depth.

Food is utilitarian, but the priority of the lunch box is given to beauty.

The soloist wins by influencing individuals, one after the other, not whole groups. More than likely you will have one supporter inside an organisation, and that person will fight for you. If you realise your impact is on individuals, not teams of people, you can and should make yourself an instrument of beauty and surprise. Learn a lot so you can share a lot. Make your knowledge diverse and deep. Go out on experimental trials. Take unusual trips. Learn things that others would love to do. And talk about it. Make yourself a treasure house of surprises.

LESSON FROM THE BONSAI MASTER

If something is true in nature, it's often true in work and life. The secrets of miniaturisation are held in the biology of miniaturisation, whose specialists are bonsai artists and growers. Bonsai artists are more difficult to capture than cat burglars. They hold their secrets as tightly as magicians hold theirs. They prefer to keep their craft to themselves. Peter Del Tredici, who curates the spectacular bonsai exhibit at Harvard University's Arnold Arboretum, was the rare bonsai master who agreed to talk about the practice of reducing a mighty tree into a creation that could fit the palm of one's hand.

Del Tredici is by training not an artist but a botanist who has studied the biology of small plants. A bonsai has a parallel life to that of a soloist. A tree that was meant to be "backdrop" in a huge forest is transformed into a work of art—a focal point—by patient effort, through the process of miniaturising it.

In nature, the miniaturised life is not just one of complexity and artistry. "Bonsai reach an immortality that humans can never hope to accomplish. The techniques of bonsai—the relentless pruning—brings about a suspension of the aging process." There is no known biological reason to believe that soloists live longer, but then there are no studies to prove that they don't.

"It is even possible in some cases," says Del Tredici, "to reverse the aging process, not just stop it. We have taken some plants back to seeds."

What if humans were psychologically, economically, socially to attempt to cut back our work scale? Would we reap some of the benefit of the immortal bonsai? Could we in our minds, or in our creations, achieve a kind of immortality not permitted to the manager or leader? Is there something intrinsically healthier about the solo life?

Two developments encourage the mad belief that the parallels with the bonsai and the soloist have some credibility. One is that every fresh-minted soloist I've seen suddenly looks much younger than when he was at work inside the corporation. Second is the maverick approach Dr. Judah Folkman is taking to the treatment of cancers, which are the epitome of reckless growth. Folkman believes killing the errant cells with chemotherapy is the wrong treatment, because it destroys healthy cells. He is achieving optimistic results by starving tumors, by cutting off their blood supply. Bonsai artists take a similar approach: Del Tredici snips at the root ball of a plant in a painstaking three-hour process so that the roots do not strangle the plant.

Says Del Tredici: "You prune a plant, and that stimulates it to put its energy into defense mechanisms. Shift from growth to defenses and the plant stays alive longer. Plants that live on top of mountains live longest. The stress of on top of the mountain forces the plant to put its energy into defenses."

It's not just that small is not just beautiful. It is the form in which longevity takes place. As in the Japanese lunch box, the *contained* is the source of its beauty. Limits force creativity to flower. It may perhaps be true that the soloist, like the bonsai plant, can have a healthier and happier work and life by self-pruning, not just by leaving the company, but by leaving the company set.

BIG OPPORTUNITIES FOR SOLOISTS NOW AND IN THE FUTURE

Solo opportunities exist in every area, but especially in one-person endeavours in the information economy:

packagers of information, Web designers, deal makers. Soloists are thriving by doing traditional occupations—like selling—on the Web. Any area in which companies are too big, or services and products need a special spin, a unique touch—that's where you find a market for solo services. Especially if you make yourself noticed as an individual: distinct, contained, in touch with the essence of work.

DOWNSCALING IS NOT DOWNSIZING

Do you become a different person when you spend time in a small world? Do you lose any effectiveness? I asked Avram if he thought I'd changed in the time I'd become a solo. He said, "There is less urgency about you." I have slowed down, but my intensity over projects has grown. I rush around much less after leads, because I need to take on fewer assignments to support myself. The impact I can have is, after all, in depth, not in scale. What I've gained on a personal level from this is an ability to pick and choose assignments: If you're going in deep on project, you want to be sure this is something that captures your spirit. I am learning how deep and diverse work is. I am learning a little of what one person can do, a potential which is often masked when you are an ant in an ant colony called the corporation.

If anything, my ambitions have grown as they have become more contained and intense. I no longer want to build a company; I want to create a work of art. That's not as mystical as it sounds. An investor said to me, "I used to chase down dozens of deals. I wanted to do them all. Now I want to do only a few deals, and do them elegantly."

Solo is singular. Not a small anything.

7. Doing Work That Matters

What is scale for the soloist? In one word, it's *projects*.

I can't remember when work didn't mean being efficient, organised, and having all the problems strategically thought through from the widest perspective. Efficient. Disciplined. That's what I thought my new work needed, same as my old work. I tried to be that way for weeks once I got my soloing papers. I carefully put my bunny slippers away every morning. Got dressed in my business girl clothes. Scheduled meetings. Eventually I started getting assignments. The assignments were not "oversee this" or "handle that." The assignments were all projects. Projects are the high art of soloing.

Efficiency was not called for. Objectivity and detachment were not prized. A grand point of view was not as important as a small tight focus on a matter. Even passion and commitment did not seem to be as effective as abject love and devotion to a topic. I entered the projects, and from there on I did not emerge in any way that was recognizable to the old me.

Work became something different and new, and I had to become different and new to keep up.

The projects are the houses of art. You enter them, and you become *of* them. You become experimental, dishevelled. You begin not entirely knowing what you're looking for, only the chance to do something great. I took on an assignment from Peter, who is developing a new leadership school, and time stopped, everything stopped, for the project. Later I went out to study Darwinism both for a magazine article and for a client who wants information about evolutionary systems and ideas. When Avram says from across a dinner table, "You have that faraway look, what are you thinking?" I forget to say, "I'm thinking about you." I say, "I'm thinking about why genes influence behavior, not just big noses and blue eyes." In the projects, you get to do something really sinful: You get to fall in love with ideas and questions. You get to work inside a tight framework. You get to end your work in a state of total self-disgust at all the compromises you've made to reach your deadline. And then when the next one comes along you can't wait for more.

This is life in the projects. That's where artists reside. Painters do projects: a canvas, in a frame. Mozart did projects: symphonies. Architects build buildings. What all these creations have in common with work you do as a solo is: You start with only a vague sense of knowing where you are going, and this is good because you want to exceed all known bounds. You want the project to transform you—whether it is composing a report, giving a speech, researching an analysis. You enter a world that is dangerous, dark, forbidding: the imagination. "Projects" is a terrible name for the high art of work, but it is a name that is true to the process. You immerse yourself. You put yourself at risk. The result is work that is deep, unsettling, and provocative.

Projects, like their urban namesake—those rickety housing complexes—are diverse, risky, immersive. That is what an artist feels like when entering the dark houses of the soul, which is where you go when you start this kind of work. You are not managing anymore, you are not overseeing others' projects. You are *in* them. "I'm a participant now as a soloist, not an observer," said Matt Owens, a twenty-eight-year-old graphics designer who left a thirty-person firm because the teamwork made each project too remote. The work of people in offices is increasingly removed from project work, and that is where the excitement is.

Projects are not products or services but a third order of work that resembles both but behaves by its own rules. For example, Avram gets a question from one of his CEO clients—how much media attention serves a company visionary vs. is it best to work by stealth: the Bill Gates model vs. the guys who pay to keep their names out of the papers. Avram is suddenly forced to consider a question that had never occurred to him before, but that has an impact on how he conducts his own life and reputation. So he begins a project: He talks to people who have faced this question. He scans vintage biographies of *Time* magazine founder Henry Luce and others who stood behind their creations, masterminding their visions but not at the expense or confusion of all their beliefs. He goes deep, into the shadows of information, not the lights and brights and flash card stuff of the Internet.

His job, in this new project, is to uncover depths. He turns the question on himself, asking: "What do I want of *my* career: to be acknowledged and applauded, or to work below the radar screen because that's where the really influential work gets done, out of the public gaze?" The very question has set him off on a search. Reaching the answer is his project, and his project is himself, because whatever he discovers, it will change not only his client. It will transform him.

"Why should a painter work if he is not transformed by his own painting," asked French philosopher Michel Foucault. So it is for all of us who live in the projects.

And at the end, Avram will have a report. He will also have research material that is his own, which he can use in a few speeches and in other consulting.

Does it sound reckless and self-congratulatory to suggest one turn soloing into a high art? No. It's necessary to conceive of some solo work as a high art. Good enough was enough when you were part of a faceless organisation. It isn't enough any more. Not when your name is on your work. Not when you can finally get the recognition you deserve. Not when there is nobody to blame but you. If everything you create reflects you, shouldn't it be terrific?

Projects are great because they teach you, because they touch the client, because they transform you both. But they are also commercially great for the soloist because you can take your work on the project, rethink it, repackage it, and resell it. Project work gives you a body of work that is in part your own.

Knowing how project masters shape projects and are shaped by them is useful. The more one is aware of the design and craft of project work, the more one gets out of the effort.

LONG HOURS, TOUGH WORK, OBSESSIVE COMMITMENT: THIS IS FUN?

No one ever said it is fun. Projects are beyond fun. This is not work hard, play hard. This is work hard, discover who you are, work hard, love every minute, work hard, come up for air. We use the word transcendent. We use the word transforming. A project teaches you who you are, at heart, because it calls up so much effort from you. A project is a deepening experience. A friend once gave me the poems of St. John of the Cross. Here was a man who made himself his own project. He was an ordinary guy who wanted to be a saint. He decided one way to do this was to lock himself inside a broom cupboard for something like thirty days. Alone and in the dark he believed he would find God. That is a project where the canvas or clay is the self. St. John coined the phrase, "the lucky dark."

"The lucky dark" is the perfect phrase for the soloist engaged in project work. Whether the task is a report or a speech, a project is not a job. It is an effort or an adventure bound in time, framed and specific but not controlled in the sense that you never know where you end up.

Every painting Mark Rothko did taught him one thing: how to paint the next canvas better. Projects teach you to be better at your craft. That is ultimately how you should choose them: Do they present you with a question you need to answer for your own life and craft? Projects are so intensive that unless you believe they will answer your own questions, not just the clients', you can't afford the time and effort to take them on. They will take too much out of you. You will give the client your best when the question is one that fires you up as well. This self-reflexive state makes projects different from any other kind of work.

Every book John Steinbeck wrote was meant to deliver a text *and* heal his vision or inform it at the same time. "By doing projects," says Jay Kernis, a producer at *60 Minutes*, you can get closer to creating something that is not just functional but that qualifies as a work of art.

Maybe you need to find new outlets for your interest in taxes and fiscal policy. Working on tax assignments only doesn't allow for deeper investigation. So you give yourself a project: to explore new tax proposals and create a booklet of your findings. In the project, you talk about who you are and why you are engaged in this search. The clients want to know something about whom they are working with. You must be on display along with the question you are pursuing. Or, say you want to venture into a new market: to work as a political strategist. Set up a project on voter habits, done perhaps as a small-scale neighbourhood study, or a film of residents on one block, perhaps it is your neighbourhood? What was your experience in studying it? The project is often best when some element of it is personal.

How do you take an idea and develop it into a project? You hone your skills, first of all.

WHO DO YOU HAVE TO BE TO LIVE IN THE PROJECTS?

Living in the projects requires a certain set of competencies:

Curiosity. Keep a constant watch on the world and yourself. Trust your instincts: If a question or topic interests you, begin exploring it on your own. This competency involves knowing how to establish that link. Alfred Sloan, the former head of General Motors and the founder of centralised management, extolled the opposite: objectivity, keeping oneself so far out of a project that it turned into pure process. Sloan said that he wanted managers who had no emotional tie to the task at hand. "No one wants a surgeon who will bleed over the patient," he said. But soloists have deeply personal feelings for their work which they shouldn't suppress.

When the U.S. military was still in the missile-making business, it was known that there was a point at which computer modelling could not determine the accuracy of a warhead. For that, what was needed was one of the old-time craftsmen to inspect the curve of the warhead visually. Missile artisans? This worried the planners who were tasked with the effort of downscaling the military, because these artisans were among the first to be forcibly retired. Once they were gone, the art would be extinguished. Some soloists have knowledge so deep it's metabolic. It's personal. They constantly bleed over their patients.

The ability to work without adult supervision. Nobody tells you how to do projects. There are certain jobs in America where you deal with what's in the in-box. Or you make the product every day and do it the same way until somebody tells you to make it red. With a project you always have to think, "What's next?"

Self-motivation. You have to judge your own work and know when something is not right, or could be better.

A thick skin. At any moment, somebody will say, "This may not be good enough, make it better." You have to know the criticism is not about you personally. The minute one removes oneself from process work for project work, one becomes willing to be judged time and again.

Ambition. You can't wait for an assignment. You have to say, "I want to do this." Hollywood is the project capital of the world. Films get made because people have a passion that defies all reason.

Egoless ego. No task is too small or unimportant in

project terms. John Steinbeck designed his own writing desk and notebooks.

Love of intensity over rationality. You have to put everything into a project. Novelist Martin Amis says, "I know that by the time I'm finished I'm completely out of gas. I'm a moron when I finish a novel. It's all in *there* and nothing's left in *here*." Same with a project of any kind.

An ability to blot out everything that is not the project. Focus. Concentration. Forgetting the big picture can be one of the most important competencies projects require. Kernis has been working with Lesley Stahl on *60 Minutes* since 1996. He lives, breathes, eats, and sleeps projects: His quota is five big stories each season from August to April. Each, he says, "has to be that extra bit special." To deliver on this, he hunkers down with samurai intensity.

"There's a lot of nonsense in life: what does somebody think of me, or am I getting what I deserve, or superficial things," he says. "When you work on projects, you have to focus and clear out those unnecessary things. Producers at *60 Minutes* have been described as being like samurai, and I ask myself, 'Am I really worthy of being one of these knights?' The job creates that culture. When you do this job you don't have time for life's nonsense. You make time for joy and fun and living. But there are people who want to mess you over, or want to gossip or create politics. That's one thing about project-oriented or lonely work. I'm not with those people."

The point at which you commit to a project, it's you vs. you. Though Kernis is part of a big corporation—CBS—he considers himself a lonely soloist in true competition only with himself.

You can be among many people. But on your project, you are solitary. The Japanese potter Hamada spoke of this kind of soloing when he was asked why he built a kiln large enough to contain 10,000 pots when he works alone and can never really use that capacity:

> If a kiln is small, I might be able to control it completely. [I can become] a master of the kiln. But man's own self is a small thing after all. When I work at the large kiln, the power of my own self becomes so feeble that I cannot control it adequately. It means that for the large kiln, the power that is beyond me is necessary. Without the mercy of such invisible power I cannot get good pieces.
>
> One of the reasons I wanted to have a large kiln is because I wanted to be a potter who works more in grace than in his own power. You know, nearly all the best old pots were done in large kilns.

"Project work is very lonely work," Jay says. "It is a monastic life and it tests what you have within you.

Some days you think, I don't know anything, or I really need to do a lot more homework. Some days you think, am I really good enough to be here? Am I as good as the other producers down the hallway?" In project work you compete only against your limitations, for the ultimate benefit of the client and yourself.

ENTER THE PROJECTS

Scouting for projects means you have to look at everything—as much news as possible, listen to as many stories as you can hear, stop talking and don't just listen. Filter everything through the focus of: Is this a potential project?

To do five projects a season, the number of extra special ones he has to produce, Kernis scans eight newspapers and a constant stream of wire copy every day, reads twenty-five magazines a month, talks with twenty publicists who call every week. He's always thinking, "Is this a story?" He doesn't turn off that filter. He considers forty or fifty story ideas in any week. He expects to consider a lot of ideas that go nowhere. "Some ideas are just perfect, but very few are."

I took one job to advise a European CEO on how to position herself for press attention in the United States. The project fit with an idea I'd long wanted to explore: the study of leadership not in terms of functions, but in terms of identity, and to look at misconceptions leaders have about who they should be. The most successful people shift identities often. They do not tend to think of themselves as consistently anything. This makes them dangerous, often frightening. George Washington, I read, needed to wear a cheap piece of ribbon on his jacket so his troops would remember him, because, many confessed, he always looked different. Maybe because he always was different. These are not matters for my client to address, but they are among of my principal ongoing questions in taking on this project. They take me to the edge of the necessity to learn a living. While I could have rejected a simple PR assignment, I saw I could develop this one into a project I would in effect be doing for the client and for myself.

To find project ideas, people keep a notebook of ideas or sometimes even phrases that catch their fancy. Maybe one out of fifty comes to fruition as a project. The act of putting these to paper gives them a seriousness, a chance to "catch" in one's mind. I start with lots of mongrel ideas, and then, when I am talking to people, I mention one or two of them. If I notice interest in the listener, I focus more attention on the idea.

Steinbeck's notebooks are fascinating documents for someone who lives in the projects. On the right-hand page, he writes the story or novel: the project. On the facing left-hand page, he writes letters to his editor that he never sends. They are more like letters to his artistic conscience about things that inspire or perturb him. The two pages are in constant dialogue: Steinbeck acting as observer/filter and creator is an effective mix. He is forced to remember what keeps him involved in the project, and that in turn makes the project fresh and sharp.

Topics can also start with the questions that are closest to your own situation. Filmmaker Woody Allen has so little downtime in a business where people spend more time not working than working because like almost every great artist, he is a prolific recycler of his life. His ideas, says Allen's biographer Eric Lax, all have some autobiographical content in that "they spring from 'a germ of experience,' that he turns and augments." If something interests you, trust it. Artists have confidence that what interests them will interest a lot of people.

The best projects grow at a "viral" rate: I consult with one client on a book he wants to write. He mentions a thinker whose ideas are, he says, "like a fine burgundy." I'm intrigued. The article that results gets me invited to conferences, and invitations to other projects. Projects handed to you this way are sometimes the best. You feel chosen for them.

Even a scrap or a word can be enough to point you in the direction of a viable project. I found Peter Senge now the world renowned visionary of the corporate learning movement, when I heard him, then a little-known lecturer, use the strange word metanoia. It was like open-sesame. Anyone who knew that word must have a head full of many fascinating things. That word led to lots of interesting projects.

IS THE IDEA WORTH A COMMITMENT?

"When a good idea first hits you, there is physiological change. It's your heartbeat, or it's goosebumps or a wave of emotion," says Jay Kernis. "There's always one other person you're telling, your wife or associate producer. As you tell what you think the story might be, you become passionate about it." That's a good test for any potential project. An idea that's so-so at the outset won't likely improve with age. "You know you are on the wrong track when there is a 'klong,' a sudden rush of shit to the heart," says Kernis.

Playwright David Mamet gets the thrill at the end, or he doesn't pursue the project. He writes plays from the end forward: He wants to know what scene theatre-goers will be leaving carrying in their heads. "Before shooting anything, you should watch the movie in your head," independent filmmaker Robert Rodriguez advises. If you can imagine the ending and love it, chances are the project has legs.

As a young writer, Henry Miller was too poor to buy the books he wanted to read. He'd wander into bookshops, look at the covers, and from there imagine the entire book. He trained himself to write entire books in his head by doing that.

You won't know all the answers to the questions your project will raise, but you can think ahead to the feeling or impact you want to create. That will help make the project real for you, and real for your client.

GO DEEP

The Internet makes every piece of information available, everything except depth. That's where a project makes its contribution: through deep research, immersion.

Look for "unaverage" clues involving very small quantities, which reveal the larger and more "average" quantities that are operating. New discoveries often reveal themselves most clearly in the workings of the smallest element.

In other words, reason from particulars to the general. Start with a story that intrigues you, like the instance of some "unique" behavior. Investigate whether this is a beginning trend. That is inductive thinking. The best project ideas begin with questions at close range, with questions that have an impact on you. Then you look around for the bigger story or issue. The reverse, reasoning from the general to the particular, is what old-school planners do. I heard about somebody investigating racial violence by studying the origins of Billie Holiday's song "Strange Fruit," about lynchings. The best way to create a project that is compelling or useful is to narrow the focus. A soloist working in a tight frame can create a compelling truth without vast reports or numbers.

Planners are trained in deductive thinking and usually try to fit particular events into laws or experiences they have had. This is in-the-box thinking. Projects afford the creator latitude to reach outside the box. Begin by observing the interactions among unique combinations of particulars.

Novelists use a small and controlled idea to branch out. When Steinbeck wrote his non-fiction book *Sea of Cortez*, after completing his magisterial *Grapes of Wrath*, "it was not the subject of the tide pool that captured his attention so much as the process of observing it," a process that "required a deep immersion into history, biology, etc," according to scholar Robert Demott.

MOMENTS OF DREAD WILL ARISE. LISTEN TO THEM

For Jay Kernis, this is when he is both excited but also questioning himself: "Do I really have a story? Use that dread to make sure you do. Along the way there might be someone who says, 'There's no story here. Oh, you've just misunderstood.'"

Whatever fears you feel, make that part of the project. Put it all into the work. Use them. Novelists try to observe how the writing of a book becomes a pattern with far-reaching consequences.

Let the process shape the work *and* reflect itself in the work. Are you on a tight deadline? If so, consider addressing the pressure in the project. Steinbeck gave himself one hundred days in which to write *The Grapes of Wrath* because he wanted to get the urgency of the writing into the story itself. If you've been given ten days to analyse and write up a corporate identity statement, that should tell you something of the pace at which identities are made, and also how long they are expected to last. The conditions of the process say a lot about the outcome of your project, the results you find.

The beauty of projects and their uniqueness as work is that they are self-reflexive. By doing them, you can examine the conditions under which the examining is done. Study the process as part of the project. Your process can be part of the very problem or trend you are investigating. Build it in.

This is not to say that a project should be your autobiography. But every painting is about the artist; every biography is an autobiography. We are our work. Acknowledge this and you can go deeper into the issues at hand. If I am consulting on the need for revised leadership identities, I had better understand why I suspect there is a need for such a study. The artist does not make something for others; he makes it for himself first and foremost. This is one-to-one marketing reduced to its essence. Something created by the self for the self: handmade to the ultimate degree. There is a hunger for such intimacy in works now.

Project designers often draft their report or presentation in the first person, in the "I" voice, even if they go back and take the "I's" out afterward. By using this personal or direct voice, they add colour, truth, and immediacy to the project.

THERE ARE DEPTHS, THEN THERE ARE DEPTHS . . .

Once they have mapped out the issues, the project designer now begins the investigative and logistical part of the project. He knows roughly where he wants to go with the idea, whom he wants to interview, and how deep he wants to drill for information. Develop the questions you want to ask your sources. Allow at least two solid weeks of research, speaking to people, checking for data on the Internet. Consider adding in a wild card source: I always ask myself, "Who is the most unlikely source I can call to reflect on the matter at hand?" In a book about soloists, for example, calling on a bonsai artist provides an imaginative depth and a different point of view.

This is the stage when the work becomes exhausting because it is now an intense gathering of data and answers. It is the hunter-gatherer phase, and it might be necessary to pull together a temporary team, much as film directors do when in production.

If one does this, how does one remain a soloist and true to a solitary or predominating vision? In my experience, the terrible thing about team projects is that they have no singular voice, so much are they the work of equality and participation. A soloist's project is dedicated to a voice and singular vision. Inviting others in to help shouldn't change that.

But be cautious. "You don't want too many partners," says film director Robert Rodriguez. "If your movie is good, you'll wonder if it was the other people that made it good; and if it's bad, it's too easy to use your partners as the scapegoats and you'll never learn anything that way."

Solos staff up temporarily by using any number of outsourcing services: researchers, information processors, secretaries, editors. You can even find experts on a free or work-for-hire basis by calling the press offices of professional associations (like the American Psychological Association for demographic help, or the World Future Organisation for trend mavens) and asking for a list of experts on your topic. Some soloists form a loose advisory board—a group of super-stringers with whom consulting arrangements have been worked out in advance. Such "on call" relationships may be paid or reciprocal.

When the data are in, it's time to start making sense of your material. Don't prejudge it. Don't say, "Oh this is no good at all." When Mark Rothko painted his all black canvases, you can bet they scared the daylights out of him. Such visions had never been committed to canvas before. They were as unformed and raw-looking as a newborn. You have to live with the project at this point. Get to know it for what it is. If it still looks ugly, maybe it is true to form and describes an unanticipated finding.

As Jay Kernis describes his work at this stage: "When we've collected maybe twenty or thirty hours of tape, I look at all that tape. I make the journalistic judgment of what tape tells the story, what tape is fair to the character. A script or report forms. You start living and breathing the script, questioning it, asking silly and serious questions about it."

REACHING FOR THE SWEET SPOT

At this point, a solution or a story or a thesis to explain the issues you're studying will begin to take shape. Then you start to judge the project. "When you get to the end," as Jay says, "you're supposed to go, 'Oh wow.'"

This is also the moment when you begin to notice

what you can't accomplish, and all the things the work will never be. Along the way, you've heard a dozen no's. People have not responded with information, time schedules haven't cooperated. "Once you're in this process it's putting blinkers on," says Jay. "You can't let yourself be stopped by the compromises. Sometimes you have to think it's a miracle you've gotten this far, because so much can go wrong.

"This is the high watermark of intensity, when you make deals with God. You want equilibrium, you want your kids to behave, you don't want bad things to happen in your personal and professional life. You need to concentrate on all these words and pictures. You want to create this smooth surface to glide over. It's a feeling of momentum and deadline approaching. It's exciting and a little scary."

The momentum takes over. The project is almost creating itself. "You feel you can do anything at this stage," Kernis says. "When you begin each project, you imagine the arrow hitting the centre of the target. Along the way we get to slow down time, as if the arrow is in slow motion. You get to do course corrections. While the world is spinning around you, you can push the arrow. You're relaxed, at peace, in the eye of the storm."

Just before you finish, you will hate the whole thing. Singers practise a song until they can't stand it anymore, until it makes them sick, they've sung it so much. That's the wall: the turning point. When they reach it, they practise the song once more, and it's theirs. They have become inseparable from it, as Yeats said, "You can't tell the dancer from the dance." Don't subvert the project too soon because you hate it. Push on.

To counterbalance this, deadlines are a must. Otherwise, a project can go on forever. A deadline makes a project the art of the possible. Understand that in any project, the possible appears to take over and the art disappears.

YOU'RE ONLY AS GOOD AS YOUR LAST PROJECT

Solos don't build a company. Instead they build a body of work. Therefore, the current project has to be better than any of the previous ones if you've succeeded. A recruiter has to keep lifting the bar on his work: making the hardest placement one time, negotiating the biggest salary the next, conducting the most interesting chase another time.

It didn't matter to Steinbeck that *The Grapes of Wrath* was one of those rare books that changed the world. *Sea of Cortez* didn't.

One way to judge your project at this point is to compare the finished product with your original proposal.

How much does it match up to that in excitement? Director Martin Scorsese said about the process of scripting *The Age of Innocence*: "We went through fourteen drafts, and we knew we were on the right track when our last draft resembled the first and second drafts more." Your initial instincts are often correct. That is when you were working with emotion and excitement as your guide. As the project goes forward, it becomes harder and harder to be original, to see things with an innocent eye.

Says Kernis: "You begin again with every piece. You have a certain technique you've developed, you have experience, but because you're challenging yourself with pieces you haven't done before, because your correspondent expects you to do that, you're in new territory every single time you walk into the screening room."

INSTEAD OF BUILDING A PRODUCT LINE OR A SERVICE, BUILD YOURSELF

The self that is formed out of a life in the projects is the artist. Soloists often not only work at a project, they watch themselves doing this work, as if from a distance, and critique their own working methods. From watching them, it's clear that some of the best of them:

Understand their own creative processes. Projects allow you to know yourself, what you are thinking. The self-reflection sharpens you in your work and in your life. You discover where your strengths are. Peter Drucker said it's a mistake for people to try to know their strengths and their weaknesses so they can attempt to turn weaknesses into strengths. Better to concentrate on improving your strengths. In the projects, you learn how to improve your strengths, discovering, for example, when you can push yourself further, and when you cannot. "I need to know when I can't do anything more this afternoon," says Jay Kernis. "That I have to sleep and the answer will come to me. You have to pray your work."

Increase their skills by imagining that they are working in another artistic medium. Novelists often imagine their book as a movie as they write. Architects imagine they are designing buildings for a world they have made. Kernis works in TV tape, but he thinks along a double track. "I'm a failed painter," he says, and so he makes painting and television into a single art in his mind, which keeps him stretching his senses and abilities. "Today I'll paint in blues so I'll do an investigative story. Yesterday I wanted to paint in reds, so I did a profile." Doing this raises the level of performance when you get too close to a project to have adequate perspective on the quality of your work.

Become adept at understanding other forms of project work. "Live theatre has helped me understand what holds an audience," Jay says. "When I go to the theatre I ask myself, 'Why am I so thrilled, what's happened here?' I listen to music for the same reason. Music doesn't go through the brain; it goes right to the soul. I ask, 'Why am I so haunted by that melody. Can a television piece transcend the medium and reach the level of art?' People manage to do it. I read the best-sellers, Grisham and Cornwell. Those are wonderful to read: characters are created very quickly and the chapters are very short." Project designers are alternately aware of themselves as artists and audiences, asking what works, what doesn't in the pop culture.

MAKING YOUR LIFE YOUR PROJECT

"Projects are controlled intensity," says Jay Kernis. The work answers a lot of the soloist's needs. Most of us go our own way, driven by enormous curiosity. We like being behind the scenes of things. Peter Drucker entitled his memoir *Reflections of a Bystander*. Projects allow us to believe that there's some filter within us that allows us to look at life and make what we observe interesting to people. "The goal of living is not to consider your work work, but to consider it your life and your play," Pulitzer Prize–winning poet Gary Snyder has said.

What's the payoff? The chance to do it all over again on another project.

8. Sell Your Soul to the Buddha You Meet on the Road

I used to divide work into two categories:

- What you had to sell your soul to do.
- What you had to do to spare your soul.

I never found a category in which I wasn't either selling my soul or buying it back. There wasn't much opportunity to keep it intact. One of my CEO bosses liked to say, "No good deed goes unpunished." In his company culture, that turned out to be true.

A person in corporate drag mostly has to hide his soul in order to save it and spare himself. Leave your soul behind you in the parking lot every morning with the car windows open just a crack. Invite the tender part of you into the office at your peril. I used to answer my phone with dread, thinking, "Oh no, another person who wants a piece of me." But a soloist takes his soul everywhere like an indestructible piece of Samsonite. A solo can sell his soul to anyone or anything, it doesn't matter. You don't have to rein yourself in any more or save the best part of you for something better. It doesn't get better than this. Diehard solos know that the more you give yourself away, the more you have. Sell it. Flaunt it. Hand it out.

And then replenish it.

There are three major sources of inspiration: objects, rituals, and authenticity.

THE CARE AND FEEDING OF THE SOLOIST'S SOUL
Objects

Objects take on a sacred value to soloists. A notebook is not just a notebook; it becomes part of you. The things in your life rise to a new level of worth. Each object has to be worth your attention. Solos move away from the strictly utilitarian. Objects are meant not only to say something about you; they have to have meaning for you. You're out of the cold corporate world where you use people and things like commodities, and you need to be reminded of that. Tools had soul to farmers. Knives had magic to hunters. Now you are living under the same set of rules as governed people who didn't work on abstract information, but who worked in direct contact with their tools, the same as artists do.

It's almost a primitive, pagan response to the world. Objects have a kind of lucky-charm worth, a talisman value. Not superstitious value, but the inspiration of the beautiful that calls you to greater expression. A solo doesn't see any disjunction between her workspace and her soul: They're connected, like a frog to a pond. A frog has no skin to protect itself, just a membrane through which the atmosphere in the pond passes nearly unfiltered. In your environment, each object has a relationship to you that is more genetic—daughterly or fatherly—than acquired.

This may be the result of having a different quality of attention to everything. You have slowed down (see the chapter "Time Is Your Real Asset") even while your life has speeded up. A race car driver could spot a rose growing out of a wall, even though he was hurtling by at 200 mph. Soloing is fast, but your attention slows down.

Perhaps solo objects take on deeper value because

you have, for the first time, control over your style; you are not given off-the-shelf supplies anymore or other corporate hand-me-downs. Solos have an almost primitive belief in the object-quality of things. Thoreau wrote a whole chapter about housing in Walden. He had very specific ideas about the shape and expense and kind of roof you need. Soloists today are inspired by things like gadgets, rituals, workspaces.

Your office is an extension of you. The cleaner your bathrooms, the clearer your head. The soloist needs to tend to the care and feeding of his soul because it's a huge resource. Here is how and what do you can do, have, or experiment with to increase your level of inspiration.

Equipment you care about helps keep you true to your vision of work. When I buy a new laptop, I stop worrying about the expense when I realise that using the newest technology improves my productivity and aesthetic appreciation.

A small 35mm camera fits this category for me. I carry it wherever I go. I take people's photos and then send them a copy to mark the occasion. My South African friend Ketan carries a tiny Nokia phone available only in Europe. He likes to use it to talk about technology and beauty and spiritual machines. It's his canvas.

Some of the most spiritual objects are signature

pieces. These are things you use and carry regularly and become known for. The young Elvis Presley felt stronger when driving from gig to gig in a pink Cadillac. He was always wrecking cars, or driving them to some mysterious early doom. He felt about pink Caddies the way I feel about my Pelikan fountain pen, which is so strange and beautiful someone's always asking to try it out.

I always carry around two books: a book I'm reading and a copy of a book I've already read and love. If someone I meet asks what I've read recently, I dig out that book and make a present of it. I love doing that because it sends me back to the bookstore on a replenishment and reconnaissance mission.

If you have an object like this that you care about in a category where you can make a present of it, you create a strong bond with another person.

Rituals

Avram makes process a ritual. Every week he schedules a meeting with himself, goes over his calendar for the last week, and asks whether the meetings he booked were worthwhile; if not, what can he learn from the bad investments in time he made? He looks ahead to the next week with an eye toward eliminating anything he agreed to do in a moment of weakness. Inside a company, a solo can take process for

Sell Your Soul to the Buddha

granted, even hate it. Then you step outside and re-alise that company process, onerous and distasteful though it might have been at times, had some benefits, like keeping you on track and giving you goals. Not every moment of your life can be self-invented. Think about the kind of process you need so work does not feel aimless.

Andrew, a Jungian therapist who works solo, says that rituals satisfy his need for routine. For a soloist, every day seems to be self-invented. The freedom that affords your work is thrilling, but it needs to be har-nessed to some events you make routine. Like e-mailing five people by noon. For Hemingway, the best ritual was stopping in mid-sentence at the end of the work-day. Leaving something unfinished helped him to get right back into work when he returned the next day. Rituals relieve the need for constant self-invention.

When you travel, make time for an assignment not on the agenda. It might be discovering something about the city or meeting one stranger. This becomes a ritual act, not a routine one. Routine is deadening. Ritual is the habit of increasing life.

Authenticity

What keeps a soloist soulfully happy? It's not just the gadgets, the books, the money, the freedom. It's the new game of business you are playing. It's the GAME ITSELF, and playing it authentically.

You may think you're the same person you were in corporate Carpet Land. And you may be. But sooner or later, you'll see by your reactions that you are playing an "infinite game," not the finite game you left behind. The infinite game runs by its own laws, which philosopher James Carse described in his cultish book *Finite and Infinite Games*.

"Whoever *must* play, cannot *play*," Carse writes. If you *must* do something, you do it in thrall to routine and need—and these conditions keep you from being playful. Finite games (which most jobs are) one *must* do. There is duress and little freedom. One cannot therefore luxuriate in the doing. In soloing, you can choose what you do to a large extent. Because you can choose to be a consultant or a writer or a photographer or a dentist, you can play at these activities. If you decide you're not the lecturer you hoped you'd be, you switch to something else. But if you fail as VP of marketing, you can't go on to be VP of finance.

Here is how Carse breaks down the difference between finite and infinite games. When you know the rules, you gain confidence in playing the bigger game, the infinite game—the solo game. That's the game that is fun. It feeds your soul.

Corporado and entrepreneurs play a finite game.	_Soloists play an infinite game._
The finite player/ corporado . . .	The infinite player/soloist . . .
is out to win.	is out to keep the game going.
is drawn to the goal (deal, success, money).	is drawn to the thrill of the play, losing all sense of self, time, and inhibition.
wants to be so perfectly skilled that nothing can surprise him, so perfectly trained that every move is foreseen at the beginning.	hopes to be surprised and doesn't mind if he loses. The game makes him better for the next round. When the surprises end, he stops playing.
plays as though the game is already in the past, according to a script whose every detail is known beforehand.	plays as though nothing is known and everything can be discovered.

Corporado and entrepreneurs play a finite game.	*Soloists play an infinite game.*
The finite player/ corporado ...	The infinite player/soloist ...
keeps his ideas close to his chest.	plays in complete openness, not as in candor but as in vulnerability. Doesn't expose his true self but rather his "ceaseless growth."
is prepared against surprise, or *trained*.	is prepared for surprise, is *educated*. The infinite player expects to be transformed by surprise
is known only by title (therefore living by routine of the job title).	is known only by his name (and therefore is self-invented: I am who I say I am).

Conduct your life by the rules of an infinite game and you can play it more naturally and happily. Carse writes:

To be playful is not to be trivial or frivolous, or to act as though nothing of consequence will happen.

On the contrary, when we are playful with each other we relate as free persons, and the relationship is open to surprise; everything that happens is of consequence.

Start playing an infinite game and opportunities show up right under your nose. Robert Rodriguez sets out to shoot a film for almost no money and can't afford props or sets. He drives along a desert road and sees a door standing open onto a desert vista, an image out of Dali. He stops to shoot a scene right there. Everything you need is right there, along the road or inside yourself. Once you realise this, you are already in the thrall of the infinite game.

It helps to take things less seriously. *Care* about your work. *Invest* yourself totally in it, as you would in any game you play. But don't take it *seriously*. If you lose a client, keep playing. Consider a setback a way to improve in playing the bigger game. Only seriousness limits fresh possibility and opportunity. "For seriousness is a dread of the unpredictable outcome of open possibility. To be serious is to press for a specified conclusion. To be playful is to allow for possibility whatever the cost to oneself," Carse writes.

Following the laws of the infinite game, a soloist is

motivated not by any definite outcome. Instead a soloist is hoping to be surprised. Also, a soloist puts his faith in something other than power. As an employee, I could only ask for what my title and job allowed. That was power. But as a soloist, my juice comes not from power but from strength.

And strength cannot be measured, Carse says. "*Power* is the freedom people have within limits, *strength* is the freedom people have without limits. Power will always be restricted to a relatively small number of selected people. Anyone can be strong." I was always afraid when I left Doubleday that no one would take my calls because I had handed in my claim on power. Now I see that those who take my calls do so because I have certain strengths, expressed sometimes as skills, other times as opinions or convictions.

The person who plays an infinite game also appears smarter and makes his clients feel smarter, because infinite games work on "open reciprocity." "If you are the genius of what you say to me, I am the genius of what I hear you say," says Carse.

SELLING YOUR SOUL

A solo pianist works close to the bone. Ben Blozan, thirty, has been soloing for four years, but it's been a steady effort to bring more of his soul onto the stage— his workspace—along with his body. He has to sell his soul to listeners. But in doing so, he doesn't deplete himself. He fulfills his expectations.

"At the beginning I didn't think I had the personality type to become a performer. I'm not the piano stud that a lot of people are. You hear that performers have to have ego, they have to want the spotlight. When I started playing solo, I would tune the audience out. Now I'm realising that when I perform I want to invite people in. I want to feel their presence. I want to know that they're there and feel like I'm helping to create this world for them.

"It takes a certain leap to do that, to go from wanting to run away to just presenting myself. For a while I didn't feel that I was enough. And maybe I wasn't enough."

Ben persisted despite performances that didn't go so well. He persisted even knowing that his musical background wasn't that strong. He played an infinite game. Despite performances that could be viewed as defeats, "I kept loving the piano more and more. I would now and then see a video of a recording of a performance of mine. I'd see how much I loved what I do. I would see how much care I put into it. I felt like, this is me. It's not something that I have to manufacture."

Playing a finite game originally, "I used to feel I would have to do ten times better than normal, or trick audiences into thinking that I'm better than I am. Now I can simply say, 'This is what I am.' I realised that even if

I didn't feel that good about a performance, people would still come up afterward and seem genuinely moved by it."

Last summer he gave a performance he didn't feel good about. "I'd gotten in my own way in that performance." Then he switched to summoning up "the courage to fall flat on my face and let that be all right. The next performance went well but I didn't feel good about the first part. I remember saying to myself, 'Just screw it. I don't care.' I started playing with a lot of abandon. I felt like I could stop anytime. It became my decision. I felt powerful in that sense, that I could to a large extent control the performance. I could cease it, I could say no."

It took pianists years to break the organisational stranglehold on playing. Blozan says, "Solo performances for piano are only about 150 years old. Before that time, court orchestras dominated and music was generally performed to commemorate big occasions. Musicians would eat with the servants and they would be treated like servants. Beethoven paved the way. He saw himself as better and above the courts, yet he could have had a very easy life if he sold out to the courts. He just couldn't work with anybody. He had to be in control."

Ultimately, solo playing is the most meaningful. "You can't fake things," says Blozan, and in soloing, you begin "learning to feel how that feels. You notice a real drain of energy when you try to do something that's not right.

"You can't fake musicianship, especially when you solo."

That is how a soloist feeds his soul: by never faking it. Playing an infinite game, you never have to sell your soul to the point of depletion.

These are the means by which you sell your soul and have it too.

Night Time

9. Rejection?

Soloing is at first a series of agonies followed by a series of ecstasies. Knowing how to deal with the tough moments makes the difference, ultimately, between success and failure.

Rejection is a keen problem for solos. X can say no to you when you're inside a company and you can pass it off. It doesn't sting. "Oh, it's not me," you think; "X doesn't like Maggie in sales." But if it's *you* someone is turning down, or ignoring, you have to take it personally.

Or you can take it more creatively.

I've met people who have bullet-proofed themselves against rejection. A business writer I know lost his father to suicide. As a result, he's grown fascinated by the reasons people soldier on in the face of adversity. It's no surprise, then, that he wrote a book about companies that last. This man Collins has one of the most dedicated plans of action for success and happiness I've ever encountered. Such an intricate plan would help spare a person the sting of rejection. Setbacks are not so devastating when the goal or the promise is big. Against it, any particular defeat seems small. It's not as if one doesn't expect rejections. But if one doesn't experience them as rejections, the harm is minimal.

Jim Moore tells a story of a Buddhist monk who woke up from a nap to teach his class. Heading toward his students, he walked clean through a huge boulder on the road. Not a scratch on him. As he approached his students, who had watched this in a state of astonishment, they asked: "How did you do that, walk through a boulder?" The monk said, "What boulder?"

Here are some ways to bullet-proof and boulder-proof yourself.

REJECTED AT THE TOP

Mona Rinzler is one of those rare and beautiful teachers who gives kids the confidence to deal with a world that doesn't care two cents about them. She taught creative writing in Passaic, New Jersey, in a school where most kids never learned to write at all. Mona offered the truest wisdom I ever heard on the subject of rejection. She said about the poems her ninth grade class was writing: "Submit them to *The New Yorker*. Start at the top. If you're rejected by the best, you can always work your way down the line. If you're rejected at the bottom, you can't move anywhere."

She might have added that if you start at the top and get your rejections *there*, you'll take yourself more seriously than if your rejections come from the bottom of the heap. If you try your luck with anybody who should be interested because they're desperate, then even an acceptance will make you feel bad. Always get rejected by the best clients. And if you play a numbers game, you're sure to hit eventually.

When you start getting rejected at the top, you find that there are a lot of people at the top, so it doesn't matter how many reject you. There's always another who might say yes.

KARMA SUTRA

Soloists go through ratty phases of the rejection that doesn't even speak its name: rejection in which you don't even rate a no. You rate no response at all. Contacts don't call back. They turn a blind eye to your proposal. Show up at a party to meet X, who asked to meet you there. But X doesn't show. All these rejections and your first thought is, "What have I done? Has my karma gone bad?"

Popularity runs in cycles. Actors lament when they're called "overnight sensations" after having worked in bone-chilling anonymity for years. The actor Dudley Moore, who scored a big hit in the movie *10*, put this into perspective. "People used to say when I showed up for auditions, 'Who's Dudley Moore?' When *10* was a hit, those same people would say 'Get me Dudley Moore!' A year later when I was even hotter, they were saying 'Get me someone *like* Dudley Moore.' Now they say, 'Who's Dudley Moore?'"

You can be hot, and then cool, then hot again. In the shade, what do you do? Do you turn up the heat, increase your output, and spread your risks? Do you back off for a time? Soloists keep on experimenting, learning, putting themselves into situations where they keep changing. They try never to get into a Dudley Moore habit of being known for one thing, one role.

BE THE FIRST ON YOUR BLOCK TO SAY NO

Bill Drenttel, the adman/designer/book producer, takes a pro-active approach to rejection. "I've always been able to walk away from a client that screamed at me. If you can walk away in the service business, it changes your life. If you did it once, you can do it again." I take it from Drenttel's words that knowing you yourself have the power to reject clients steels you against the bumming-out effects of rejection of you.

THE MIND OF THE NAY-SAYER

When I am rejected, I try to think my way into the rejecter's mind. I try to see myself as the other person sees me or my work. Maybe I appeared too flighty. Maybe I gave the impression I didn't care enough. Maybe the project I thought was great really sucked.

But I also think historically. I find that people reject someone in the same way in which they perceive that they were once rejected—perhaps even by you. If you said something brash to them a year ago, you'll find it echoed in their rejection of you. Since the world is only becoming smaller, this is a real issue. You will have to say no sometime to someone, but beware: You'll get it back. The lesson: Be careful what you do to others. It will be done unto you. Philosopher Simone Weil noted that people try to hurt others by passing on the blows rather than containing them. It takes a tremendous amount of courage to let the hurt another person inflicts end with you. That she did it qualified her as a saint in many eyes.

If I don't know the rejecter, I try to analyse the situation structurally. Was it a particular type of assignment/meeting/personality that I have had a bad experience with before? If so, might there be some damaging subliminal response I have in these kinds of situations that disqualifies me immediately? For example, some soloists are not as effective in a group as in a one-on-one meeting, and many rejections occur there. It's important to know what conditions reject you before you even walk into the room.

REJECTED FOR YOUR SUCCESS

Perhaps the worst thing is to be rejected by people *because you've done well*, not because you've disappointed them. That can sting more than rejection by people who have a right and just cause in rejecting you.

I'd heard complaints from people who say my solo life has been easy. They choose to believe that I had and have contacts in powerful places, when in fact I left publishing books behind and wasn't known for my solo occupations—journalism and consulting. Of the dozens of authors I'd helped to write best-sellers and make millions, not one of them offered help in return.

To get over being rejected for your success, avoid mistaking it for rejection. Some people will feel diminished no matter what and try to make you their scapegoat. You buy in to their biases at great cost to your belief in yourself. You can come to think as they do that you don't deserve your success.

Executive consultant Tracy Goss takes a very healthy approach to these cases. She explains that people routinely try to "hook" you. They offer withering opinions, and your mistake is to think these opinions have some merit, when in fact they are only opinions. Would you allow someone who berates you, for example, to perform surgery on you? No? Then why would you trust one of them to get under your skin and alter how you feel about yourself? Most people don't know you, and certainly don't know your situation. They are as ill-qualified to deliver an opinion of you as they are to repair your heart.

That's how other people get power over you: by dishing out ill-informed opinions. People are full of opinions, and if you start listening to them, you're doomed. Mostly, they are projecting their own failures onto you. Few people, except those to whom you are close, know you well enough to criticise you. Forget the others. Stay busy, stay in love with your work, and others' rejections—their hooks—won't sink into you.

WHEN YOU JUST WISH SOMEONE WOULD LAUGH AT YOU

The old *Cheers* sitcom song goes: "You want to go where everybody knows you name . . ." and so you do. Except those people are not here right now. Everybody who *is* here is looking at you as if you got in by bribing the doorman. Do you feel like you don't belong? Group rejection is a bummer, and solos often find themselves at parties and conferences where, if their name tag doesn't identify them as one of the Big Ten, they are made to feel invisible.

Futurist and veteran conference goer Paul Saffo has a theory of how to behave at big parties if they scare you: Stand in one place the whole night. Everybody you need to see will pass by you, and you'll get to talk to everyone without trying to edge in on groups and feeling rejected when no one makes a space for you because you are not one of them.

A newly minted solo may have trouble getting seen and heard. For that, there is a solution. When he was a young up-and-comer at Disney, Jeff Katzenberg, now CEO of Dreamworks, was determined to break into Hollywood's inner circle. Katzenberg would call the secretary of a real mogul every half-hour, sounding as sweet and charming on the twentieth try as on the second. That was the key: Sound sweet each time. You make it clear that rejection simply doesn't stop you. Not because you are a bully, but because the arrows bounce off your skin.

Finally the secretary, who was beside herself with this sweet maniac, begged her boss to take the call just to end her torment. Every rejection was just another opportunity for Katzenberg to break through.

Cleopatra got an audience with emperor Julius Caesar by having herself rolled up inside a magnificent Persian carpet and delivered to the palace. When the emperor's minions unrolled the rug, she popped out in all her splendour. Taking a page from Cleopatra, marketing consultant Don Peppers once found out where a perpetually rejecting client was holding a meeting at a hotel. Before the lunch was scheduled to be served by the hotel waiters, Don picked up steaming hot pizzas and delivered them himself to the conference room. The guests, who were not looking forward to the hotel lunch, were so grateful for the pizzas that they invited him to make them a business proposal. They ended up hiring him, reversing years of rejection.

WHEN IT FEELS GOOD TO DO THE REJECTING

Let's get back to Bill Drenttel's claim that rejecting offers yourself helps you deal with your own rejection.

Get an offer, and your first response will be such relief that you'll grab at the deal. You'll grab at anything. Which means that soon you'll have grabbed at everything.

People want you. Isn't that great? Not necessarily. Because the more you take what comes, the less available you'll be when the big "stretch" assignments roll in. In the solo world, getting a reputation for turning down some business enhances your attractiveness. When people hear no, they want to offer you more money.

Before taking a job for the money, consider what it is really worth. If you are offered £5,000 for a speech,

163

that may sound fine. But is it worth two days of traveling, because in after-tax money, it represents only £3,000. Weigh every yes by this measure. Ask yourself if a year from now, will you be glad you did this project, or will you have forgotten it? If the latter, why commit to it at all?

But be careful not to reject business you've already accepted. Be cautious of getting into situations where you have to reject others. Remember: What you do will be done to you. I recently overcommitted myself to projects, and then had to reject some of them. Not cool. I may never see these clients again.

AMAZON.COM

"Write about women," a friend said. "We have special trouble going solo. Independence is scarier for us." It's true. Women go through girlhood as strong, independent creatures. Then they hit adolescence and behave as if they were born to be dependent: on a man, a job, a system. Women loathe being rejected, so soloing is twice as offputting.

Men who solo are heroes. John Wayne rode into town a stranger and left a stranger. But lone women feel they bear the mark of rejection. Few women are invited to go unaccompanied to dinner parties, where a lot of social business is conducted. Lone women don't help women very much. It's only gotten worse since

Monica Lewinsky, who unleashed jealousy and suspicion, which one woman summarised in a simple line: "What woman will ever let her husband alone with Monica for a job interview?"

There have been a lot of accolades pressed on women entrepreneurs and women who break the glass ceiling to lead Fortune 500 companies. But women who go solo defy *all* the odds, statistical, emotional, and social.

Break away from the corporation, and you are orphaned. If you are also single, being solo means defying every belief that someone will take care of you. With no shield around you, every rejection seems a personal slight.

It is a personal slight. All business is personal. But you don't need to work with everybody. And a lot of clients will welcome you because as a woman on your own it's assumed by those in the know that you're twice as strong, good, and sensitive as anyone else. I take heart from the phrase Somali women use: "Onions are my husband." Economic self-sufficiency, they mean, is the relationship of the independence.

ONE HUNDRED PERCENT BULLET-PROOF

You can actually make yourself rejection-proof by reacting to rejection with enormous generosity. Write a thank-you note to the person rejecting you. Send a gift or something that you think will benefit that person and a letter saying you are grateful to have met X and for the insight he's given you. Don't mention future business at all. This is essentially what Gandhi did: He loved his enemies the British until they finally yielded to his desires and agenda. People can't muster anger or hurtfulness in the face of generosity. You win more effectively by love than by war.

Lots of artists believe that unless they are rejected frequently, they are not working hard enough. If you start getting too few rejections, it's a sign you are protecting yourself, that you are not reaching high enough or going far enough. If you land one opportunity for every ten rejections, you are doing fine.

There are so many reasons to be thrilled with soloing that rejections can't be accorded much seriousness. Reject rejection and nothing will stop you.

10. So Alone

The essential element in soloing is aloneness. You can worry about everything else in
advance—identity, money, time. But you
can't be prepared for how alone you will feel.
The world is so full of human DNA that we
take other people for granted. But put yourself alone at a desk and you can't believe how
quiet it gets. If you can appreciate the value
aloneness brings to your work and to your development as a soloist, you gain enlightenment from it.

In a conversation with Joseph Campbell on
the power of myth, journalist Bill Moyers
noted:

There is a haunting incident in the story of Odysseus,
when the ship tears apart and the members of the crew
are thrown overboard, and the waves toss Odysseus
over. He clings to the mast and finally lands on shore
and the text says, "Alone at last. Alone at last."

Moyers wanted to know why a brave hero who had fought fearlessly alongside his men would be so grateful to be alone. Campbell explained that Odysseus recognised this moment as a chance to realise full enlightenment. Odysseus rejoices in the aloneness even though he eventually comes back to society.

Odysseus knew the value of comradeship and friendship on the Greek battlefield. But alone and lost at sea, he would discover what *he,* not the Trojan armies, was made of. Aloneness teaches a person what is essential in life. Prison memoirs from those of former South African president Nelson Mandela to those of writer Oscar Wilde are filled with self-discovery and an experience of the overwhelming power of the individual.

We live our lives in relationships, and to tear open this fabric and experience aloneness invites you to discover a new plateau for yourself. A child is sent alone out of the tribe for a period of time—a test—by which he becomes an adult. A soloist experiences in aloneness an absence of the familiar comforts in the presence of others that will hold him back. That is why on the hero's journey, the world drops away. Heroes need to experience aloneness *and* understand what it does for them.

Campbell said, "Almost all the old Greek cities were founded by heroes who went off on quests and had surprising adventures, out of which each then founded a city. You might also say that the founder of a life—your life or mine, if we live our own lives, instead of imitating everybody else's life—comes from a quest as well."

Nelson Mandela said that prison forced him to rely on no strength but his own. He could lean on no one. At Robben Island, the prison colony off Cape Town, food was rationed, and work was servitude. Still, these were nothing compared to the feeling of being cut off from family and friends.

> I found solitary confinement the most forbidding aspect of prison life. There is no end and no beginning; there is only one's own mind, which can begin to play tricks. Was that a dream or did it really happen? One begins to question everything. Did I make the right decision, was my sacrifice worth it? In solitary there is no distraction from these haunting questions. Strong convictions are the secret of surviving deprivation; your spirit can be full even when your stomach is empty.

Soloing is not on the same level as Mandela's trials. Still, there is something to be learned from his words, because the quality of aloneness one feels is thick, like a deep fog that isolates house from house, body from body. You don't simply feel alone in those first weeks, you feel stripped without the essentials you have relied on: someone to take your calls; a conversation with a colleague; an associate who knows the people you know. Solo, you are cut off from this community. You are following your own way, not your company's. And until you know what that way is, you can feel like a stranger to yourself.

Soloists tend to have more than the average human need for solitude, and while this should protect them, it actually exposes them. You think you can handle the solitude, which means you may let it increase its hold. "Solo," Avram said, "sometimes sounds like so-low."

Aloneness can seem like an enemy until you stop fighting it, at which point it mysteriously turns into a friend. Everyone knows stories of people who have lived very regimented lives. Anointed early to high corporate positions, they have lived by the rules of their position. Then something happens to shake up their world. Their company changes hands, they are fired, a divorce or illness or death comes their way. They have a difficult time, but perhaps they survive the turmoil brilliantly and gain the will of a saint. They become stronger and more humble. The Dalai Lama is like this. The lesson is, "Love thine enemies," because the strengths they call up in us make them the instruments of our destiny.

Love the loneliness and you realise there is a basic element of soloing that has to be done apart. The solitude strengthens you, gives you the chance to listen to yourself. When your own voice sharpens, so does your performance. You know your thoughts, which makes you a better consultant, artist, etc. Originality is what the world hungers for, and having set out by yourself, you have bought into this belief system.

The soloist faces not just aloneness, but profound and unbroken patches of solitude, where you drift into your mind as if into a dream. In that depth you not only work, you change. You grow.

THE JOURNEY INWARD

The art of working alone is not something we instinctively know how to do. Most all work is social; it is done in teams. Michael Jordan was told, "There is no 'I' in team." "But there is an 'I' in win," he said.

When you decide to solo, to stand apart, you choose aloneness.

When Charles Lindbergh had the dream to fly across the Atlantic, he was hardly the first. More than seventy people had already crossed over, all members of flying teams who made it across only in stages. If you are alone, risk doesn't seem so risky. Alone, a person is willing to take on a bigger assignment. "I'll fly alone," Lindbergh said. "That will cut out the need for any selection of crew, or quarreling."

Lindbergh was so intent on testing himself against only himself that even the fabric in the plane proved too much companionship for him. "If there's upholstery in the cabin, I'll tear it out for the flight. I'll take only the food I need to eat, and a few concentrated rations . . ."

Solitude, said poet Joseph Brodsky, is "like being in exile. One of the advantages is that you shed lots of illusions. Not illusions about the world, but illusions about yourself. You kind of winnow yourself. I never had as clear a notion of what I am than I acquired when I came to the United States—the solitary situation. I like the idea of isolation. I like the reality of it. You realise what you are."

Simplicity, knowing yourself, that's the work of solitude. It is a job in itself. What you learn through solitude is whether you are a match for your task

"Lindbergh Flies Alone," became the headline of the most famous newspaper story of its era. The reporter who wrote it asked how anyone could consider himself alone with courage, skill, and faith in the cabin with him. That's not just some feel-good platitude. Belief in yourself peoples your space.

Lindbergh often thought he wasn't alone on that flight. He hesitated to talk about it, and only three decades later would he publicly discuss how twenty-four hours into his ordeal "the fuselage behind him filled with phantoms—vaguely outlined forms, transparent, moving, riding weightless with me in the plane." They appeared through the fabric walls of the plane. They spoke to him in human voices above the noise of the engine, giving him "messages of importance unattainable in ordinary life," according to his biographer Scott Berg.

Eerie, except if you think of Lindbergh's experience as a dream. The voices may have been his own voice suppressed in his ordinary life. The kind of voice that led Coleridge to write "Kubla Khan," or that led Picasso to paint *Les Demoiselles d' Avignon*, working locked away, alone and naked in his basement studio. It was how he exorcised his feelings into the powerful visions on canvas.

Work alone and your essence as a human being is drawn out. People are looking for an experience of the world "that will open to us the transcendent that informs it and at the same time forms ourselves within it. That is what the soul asks for," says Campbell.

The magic of soloing is soloing.

This is not to say that the soloist needs to walk to the same edge as Picasso, Coleridge, or Lindbergh. It is to say that the aloneness is a testing ground. If you don't fear it, if you don't interrupt it with a call to AT&T to surreptitiously ask if your phone is working, then you will get more out of the solo experience.

Lindbergh's solo flight changed the pilot. It also changed the planet. He came out of the flight free to take on missions in everything: medicine, physics, and politics. He'd broken through the barriers in his own life and was on his next solo excursion, free to try everything.

WHEN ALONENESS BECOMES TOO MUCH

One of the consequences of working alone is the loss of perspective. Little problems build into big ones. Churchill called depression the black dog. A small slight grows into a big one. Why is depression often tied to being alone? Because you lose perspective on what's important. What to do about it?

It helps to remember that any day you have as a soloist is better than any day you had as a corporado. It helps too to make a commitment to something: Attachment rescues you from the state of solitariness.

To be alone is to realise an essential cut-to-the-bone truth about existence, one we usually paper over, one that the solo experience exposes: that aloneness is the essential human condition. We live in families, we work in groups, but ultimately we are each responsible for ourselves. That more than anything makes man free.

Soloing is tough and exhilarating; the tougher it is, the more exhilarating it is. Be prepared for the aloneness, but don't fight it. Don't wish it away. It is the ground on which you are tested most.

11. F Dover

There is rejection and there is loneliness in every soloist's career. And then there is the one place where they come together. That is called F Dover, a particular spot in hell.

I usually wind up there at some point on every solo mission. Sometimes I arrive when an editor pal calls after weeks of silence to tell me that he's handed me off to someone else who also won't call for three weeks going on three months. Or I make a superhuman effort to get down to a Washington, D.C., meeting organised by one Jill N., devoting a whole day to her, gratis, only to get stiffed on the promised expenses.

In F Dover waiters serve cold food warm

and warm food cold, and never the dish you ordered. Other native conventions: You are promised but not paid. You are manipulated or guilt-tripped into doing something you know runs counter to your best interests. The nicest people with the deepest dimples are often the ones who offer you a free first-class ticket to F Dover. We've all been there. What do you do when you seem to be in a frequent flyer circuit to that little piece of hell?

There are many emotions you can't afford to have as a soloist. Like anger, frustration, revenge. You become a better lover, friend, parent, and spouse because soloing forces you to deal with yourself. In a corporate setting, you become a child. Ma-Pa corporation breeds the sense that whining and vengeance and other politics are okay. Soloing is a quick lesson in adulthood. You go into a Zen-like state when you realise you create your world, and are responsible for your creation. You take responsibility for the good and the bad.

And here's where it really comes in handy. You don't have time for negative emotions.

What's more, if somebody fucks you over *and* you feel fucked over, you make that person powerful.

I draw one distinction when I get to F Dover. Is this relationship worth saving? Or do I need a lawyer? My answer is: Every relationship to a soloist is worth saving. Because you are alone, you never know whom you will need when. I say this having unplugged many relationships I wish I'd put on life support.

Forgiveness is a wonderful emotion. It's actually even nicer for the forgiver than for the forgiven. It gives you a sense of control and largesse. Remember that when it seems as if only a total case of method acting will ever bring the forgiveness feeling back.

Instead of getting mad, write a letter of sympathy. Tell Barbie's evil sister, the Jill Doll who stiffed you, that you have tried to get your expenses paid, as she promised. But you realise it may be difficult for her to live up to such a generous offer. Delete the snide "generous," and then suggest you will do a fund-raiser for her when you are next in town. You will, perhaps, turn a bad relationship into a good one. In any case, this will pop the bubble of your anger. And you won't waste time in planning revenge. Even if the revenge is terribly clever. Jay Chiat, founder of the ad agency Chiat-Day, liked revenge with style. If someone wasn't making good on a promise or commitment and refusing his calls, Chiat would telephone that person's secretary and say, "Tell X that it's Dr. Schwartz calling with the results of his tests."

Know that every company, from the biggest to the smallest, plans for visits to F Dover. They call it Bad Debt. Don't have the idea that everyone will pay you what they owe. "A company the size of Intel will plan on bad debt as low as one per cent," says Avram. "But a small company that does business with other small companies can sometimes carry a bad debt rate of 10 per cent. That's high, but by planning for some number, you won't be so hurt by debt that isn't paid."

The higher you lift your head, the more stuff is dumped on it. In Australia they call this "the tall poppy syndrome." The tallest poppy gets raped by the wind, rain, and garden shears. Expect rejection, criticism, lack of understanding. Writers say they never read their reviews—good and bad. If they are sucked in by the praise, they'll also have to believe the criticism.

Niccolo Machiavelli warned the prince that the danger of flattery is second only to the danger of war. Flatterers are pests, because they carry deceit. Some princes guard themselves against flattery by letting people understand "that the truth does not offend you." But that opens you to ridiculous comments as well. Therefore, says Niccolo, choose only a handful of people you trust and "give them the liberty of speaking the truth to you," but form your own conclusions. Outside of these trusted counsellors, listen to no one and "be steadfast in this."

F Dover is a place that will always pull you back, like the worst version of home on a wet, not white, Christmas. Remember one thing, ye hearty soloist: In real terms *you are alone*. And at this moment, this is really good news, as good as it gets. Because you've just made the whole world up. They're not really there. The Dolls, the Opinionizers, the Gardeners with their tall poppy shears. It's just YOU in your world. Get on with your life. Live it as if it's the last day and be thrilled to have one more chance to do what YOU want.

F Dover

Daybreak

12. When Thoreau Left the Lights on at Walden Pond

A year ago a stranger asked me, when she learned what I did, "What will you do when soloing gets old?" I was taken aback. Has an executive ever been asked what he'll do when managing gets old? This stranger had the strange notion that no one solos for the long haul.

I couldn't imagine a year into this life that I'd ever do anything but solo. Now two years into the role, I am wondering if soloing is a transition to something else. Going solo is one of the best things one can do to deepen one's knowledge and identity. It's a bold and testing experiment. But I am not sure it is a lasting state.

Henry David Thoreau left Walden Pond abruptly after a two-year experiment. He had gone there in 1845 to prove to himself and others that a person could be independent. He believed that his hometown, Concord, offered no opportunities for meaningful work. Rather than live a "desperate" life, Thoreau insisted upon living "deliberately." He built a hut with his own two hands on the pine slope against the shores of the pond. It was a hut that he furnished and kept in order entirely by the work of his own two hands. He earned his bread by doing a little surveying, performing odd jobs, and tilling a few acres for the beans and potatoes he ate. He gained absolute independence. He came to know the birds and fish and animals at Walden more intimately than St. Francis knew his. The birds sought him out, the animals caressed him, the fish glided between his hands. He read and wrote. His leaving Walden Pond and the solo life may have had something to do with his anger, during his walks, at seeing the way black Americans were treated. His sympathies were for them and probably for himself, a recognition that we are all slaves. It was this disgust that led him to refuse to pay the poll tax to a country that sanctioned slavery. For this he was arrested. He may have left the solo life to become more involved in social action. In any case, when he left Walden, he went back to his parental trade of making pencils.

He says very little about why he brought his solo life to a close. "I left the woods for as good a reason as I went there. Perhaps it seemed to me that I had several more lives to live, and could not spare any more time for that one." Walden had come to seem routine to him, the paths to and from his door now a beaten track, and he was always afraid of the depth of the "ruts of tradition and conformity."

What did he learn?

I learned this, at least, by my experiment; that if one advances confidently in the direction of his dreams, and endeavours to live the life which he has imagined, he will meet with a success unexpected in common hours. He will put some things behind, will pass an invisible boundary; new, universal, and more liberal laws will begin to establish themselves around and within him; or the old laws be expanded, and interpreted in his favour in a more liberal sense, and he will live with the licence of a higher order of beings. In proportion as he simplifies his life, the laws of the universe will appear less complex, and solitude will not be solitude, nor poverty poverty, nor weakness weakness.

And then he writes the most famous line of *Walden*: *If you have built castles in the air, your work need not be lost; that is where they should be. Now put the foundations under them.*

At Walden Pond he measured his own strength for bold action, which he says is "extravagant." The root of the word means travel (vagant) widely, well beyond one's limits (extra).

I fear chiefly lest my expression be not extra-vagant *enough, may not wander far enough beyond the narrow limits of my daily experience, so as to be adequate to the truth of which I have been convinced.* Extra vagance! *it depends on how you are yarded. The migrating buffalo, which seeks new pastures in another latitude, is not extravagant like the cow which kicks over the pail, leaps the cowyard fence and runs after her calf in milking time.*

It's clear that Thoreau identifies not with the migrating buffalo. However far the beast travels, it is still locked in the routine of its life. But the cow breaks with convention. Her leap over the fence is a bolder move though it doesn't take her far. For Thoreau, Walden Pond—soloing—is everything while the experience remains fresh, new, bold. The minute it loses this edge, the experiment is over.

"I desire to speak somewhere *without* bounds," Thoreau writes, "like a man in a waking moment, to men in their waking moments, for I am convinced that I cannot exaggerate enough even to lay the foundation of a true expression."

Even for Thoreau, the premier soloist, soloing could not fill a whole existence. *It was one passage in the art of perpetually testing the self.* When soloing became old, when it stopped being a journey, he had to move on.

But before we leave Thoreau, we must learn a few more secrets that others have come to see in his leaving. The literary critic Stanley Cavell said that leaving Walden was the same for Thoreau as entering it: a crisis. Entering and leaving were both touched off by a moment when a new commitment had to be made. You don't really leave Walden, you give it up so you can begin something new. You take its lessons with you. For "Walden" here read "soloing" in the general sense. Cavell is describing soloing as a mythic journey that goes like this: The hero throughout history leaves his hut, his familiar turf, and goes into an unknown wood from whose mysteries he wins some knowledge.

One can only solo in the largest meaning of the word, that is, with the most satisfying opportunities available. We will likely come within touching distance of them if we keep repeating this process: leaving behind the familiar.

Did Thoreau pack so quickly that he left a light burning at Walden Pond? His last line of Walden is: "The sun is but a morning star." Even the sun is a small light on a solo path.

Would I leave the solo life? Yes, if I had the conscience to know that it was getting too comfortable. If I was short-circuiting my learning and the care I took with projects. But that begs another question: What would I leave this for? What could replace the freedom and the joy of this work?

CLOSING TIME

Would someone who had tasted the freedom of soloing go back into the corporate pouch, into the corporate maw? For some people, soloing is not a permanent home. It's a transition back to where they began their careers—but at a higher level. Some of the greatest figures in the twentieth century have turned to soloing for a time, for a change in order to rehabilitate their reputation and to gain crucial skills to jump to another phase of life.

When Winston Churchill was voted out of office in disgrace as Britain's chancellor, one step away from prime minister, he took to soloing. From this solo base of writing and making speeches, he managed to re-establish a position of power. Being out of office enabled him to refresh himself, to practise his skills, and to obscure the power landscape with fresh and newly critical eyes. He achieved certainty in his political positions. Something about his withdrawal slowly made him seem a more attractive and interesting and believable figure—no small achievement because from his exile he was arguing the most unpopular views of his day! Re-engagement in war after Britain had suffered tragic losses in the First World War. Could he have come back to lead Britain through the Second World War without that hiatus when the political world could judge Churchill from a different perspective?

Perhaps he anticipated the public's fascination for returning heroes. Artists from painters to singers are sent packing in the popular imagination so they can be rediscovered and brought back to their pedestal.

It's healthy too to regard a stint in the corporate world as the interruption to their lives, and soloing the true, bedrock state of being. Michael Johnson periodically leaves the work of independent production to take on a big corporate project, in order to experiment with his ideas. Even if he fails, he knows he can always go back to soloing. So what's the risk in re-entering corporate life for one to three years?

Thoreau left Walden not because he was drawn to something else, but because he felt he had gotten all he could out of soloing. Soloists move on, sometimes, for the same reasons that Hemingway left Spain, or Henry James and Whistler left Paris. Spain and Paris were these artists' Waldens—places they could be essentially alone and apart. They tried to make a go of living in a culture they loved, which fed their individuality, but maybe because of its very intensity, they couldn't live permanently in a place that's a honey pit of a esthetic, self-searching disposition. The solo life is so exciting in part because it is romantic, a bit enclosed, a little clannish. You may eventually need a more neutral place to inhabit.

Or if the testing impulse gets to you, you leave soloing for a well-deserved rest. A friend ran her own solo business attached to a large accounting/consulting firm for five years, and then decided the overwork was too crushing. She left for a nine-to-five job, thinking of that as early retirement.

Some people solo to wait out the rough spots. The philosopher Confucius, who worked as a police chief in one of the prefectures in ancient China, would periodically leave his post whenever the administration changed, as it did frequently, and the barbarians blew into town. Confucius would retreat for the countryside and wait until the barbarians destroyed themselves. Then he returned to his job. Meantime, he waited his enemies out by writing his philosophical maxims. There is a fair amount of this temporary retreat to the sidelines going around these days. Publishing, an industry I loved for nearly two decades, has been turning sour. There was no place in its purely corporate theology another industry shift could occur. If I were free, I'd see the change coming more clearly than if I were in it. I'd be in a better position to get an early sighting of those changes and take advantage of them.

What would I want on leaving a solo life? Partners with whom to share a business experience? Or just the opposite: employees who would do what I say and serve no vision but my own?

Or would I just relax and say, "I've proven myself. Enough is enough"? If I stayed solo, I would look for a client or institution to have a long-term relationship with, and get free of the need to constantly find new business.

Perhaps I would slip even further into the solo life by writing a novel. If I do so, I will have benefited from learning how to work alone and still cope: how to pay the bills and look for interesting projects when I ran short of money or companionship.

And if I went corporate, what would I have learned? To stand my ground, to use my imagination, which the years of corporate life had bleached me of, the way the desert sun bleaches all things white and dry as dust.

How do you know you're ready to transition out of soloing? Compare your work now to what it was six months or a year into the solo life. Are you more proud of it now? If not, a change is needed.

If it's not time for a move out of soloing, what changes should you make? Look around. Talk to people. Then make some commitment, any commitment, to get you started. Or as novelist Robertson Davies suggests: "Choose what you believe and know why you believe it, because if you don't . . . , you may be certain that some belief, and probably not a very creditable one, will choose you."

You can re-enter the land of the morning star, where the clock has you marching through someone else's door at nine A.M. But once you have soloed, no one can own you. You will always be a soloist, a one-and-only.

Part 2 THE BUSINESS OF BEING YOURSELF

Harvest

13. Great Work Finds You

Consultant Jim Moore was embarrassed to admit it. I was embarrassed to admit it. The reason for our embarrassment is that we don't find great work, it finds us. To admit that sounds so above-it-all, so "let them eat peanuts while we sip champagne." As if we were bred by bobcats to pick off the goodies and leave the bones for the crows.

The truth is, opportunities will come to you. Lots of them. The difficulty, however, is in becoming a target for great work.

What is great solo work? An opportunity in which you are paid to learn. Soloing is learning, not just earning a living. You only need a few great jobs as a soloist. And you can never find them. Work like this has to find you. But there are ways to ensure that it will find you.

I've spent my adult life hunting—for jobs, for money, for clients like authors and magazine editors and CEOs to take heed of me. Nothing ever came to me free and clear, and I expected I would have to do more begging and scraping as a solo. Yes, I had a reputation. But my reputation was as an editor and publisher, not as a consultant or writer, which is the basis for my solo career. I thought I'd have to start from the bottom all over again. I was wrong. The mechanism for being hired as a solo is different from finding jobs as a corporado.

But I didn't know this at the start, so I spent my first solo year cozying up to people I desperately wanted to turn into bread-and-butter ventures. Every potential job I pushed for never materialised in the accounts-receivable column. I couldn't figure out what I was doing wrong. I was doing exactly what I'd always done. Then I realised the people to whom I didn't pay heed wooed me. Same with Jim. There is something to this, and it's not vanity. What is it?

There are a couple of reasons for this. One is that the world of organisations works by the expression of will and dominance. You push and prod with the added force of a corporation behind you, and things eventually happen. That's what clients expect. The soloist can push for things to happen, but you're not a ten-ton gorilla and so will doesn't count. Attraction counts. You make yourself visible, and you attract opportunities and clients.

Second, this is the new economy: the passing of the mass-market era one epitomized by Fred Joseph, CEO of the once powerful, now defunct investment firm Drexel Burnham Lambert. Joseph would crash strangers' weddings and bar mitzvahs every weekend, pretending to be a member of the celebrating family in order to hand out his business cards to the guests. Soloists can't capture work by these mass-market means. Nor do you need to: A solo needs the best, most adventurous clients to do work that can make a reputation—the client's and your own. And because a solo needs no more than few clients, you can choose among them as if you *were* bred by bobcats.

But the most important reason that soloists tend not to have to solicit work is that nowadays *there are more clients eager for great work and fewer producers of great work.* Ten years ago, a large number of producers competed for a limited number of consumers. You'd get brand wars: Coke and Pepsi fought with each other for market share (they still do). But in the information hierarchy, clients (aka consumers) battle one another for the time and attention of the best soloist. So Avram leaves Intel, and within a week his calendar is full. Clients are battling for his attention because talented producers are limited in number. The talented producer calls the shots, not the customer. Know this dynamic, and you save yourself a lot of wasted motion.

A new solo's energy is best spent becoming known, thus letting the client find you. "When I left Hewlett Packard," said Don Norman, "I studied books on service companies because I thought that was what I was going to be: a one-man service company. A friend gave me good advice that completely threw me: 'Your model should be Hollywood. Think of yourself not as a service provider but as a star. That's what people want. When they call you, they're not calling for product development advice. They're calling for Don Norman.'" In fact, Hollywood is the only place in the world where there is a solid infrastructure for soloists: agents, managers, lawyers all dedicated to building singular careers. In the future, the Hollywood model will be available to soloists everywhere.

There's a bonus in this approach of letting great work find you. Sign up for this psychological dynamic, and you don't work *for* the client. You work together to "co-create" a market, an idea, a project.

CO-CREATORS

Consider this basic question: What do you want from your clients? For me the aim is to partner with someone with whom I can financially or creatively build an idea or project into something bigger, something with impact. Clients (by which I mean anyone who pays you to learn) thus become partners. To establish a solo/client relationship with someone with whom you can cocreate projects, not someone who expects you to serve them slavishly, you don't simply need to be visible, says Jim Moore. "You need to establish trust."

You also need to know that although the client is paying the bills, you are the boss. In soloing you put yourself on an equal footing with people who pay the bills. That's another way in which solo work is similar to the way an artist works. The client is a patron rather than a boss.

Among history's greatest soloists were the artists of the Renaissance. Leonardo da Vinci died in the arms of his patron, Francis I of France. This testifies to client relationships that run deeper than patronage or work-for-hire arrangements.

Renaissance artists considered themselves the equals of their kings, not their employees or servants, and the kings treated them in kind. Giulio de' Medici confessed that whenever Michelangelo came to see him, "he, the Pope, made haste to sit down and to invite the sculptor to do likewise, because, if he were not quick about it, Michelangelo would take a seat anyway without asking permission," according to Mary McCarthy. Michelangelo

Great Work Finds You

did not try to impress his client. Deliberately he behaved as himself, unpolished, blunt. The sculptor liked to leave some roughness on a finished statue to show the mark of the sharp tools he had used on it, and in the same way, left the roughness on his speech and manners to show his feelings of equality.

To work at this level of enrichment doesn't take many clients. "I would like to have two great clients," Jim Moore said. "One is too few. With one you are in danger of becoming co-dependent. But a soloist doesn't need more than a few clients. I know some investment bankers who do only two deals a year. You want a diversification of neuroses.

"A great client," Jim says, "is someone who has influence, money, and wants the same things you want."

How does such a person find you? There are two ways to be noticed: first, honing your visibility, and second, developing your value-added.

HOW GREAT CLIENTS FIND YOU

Here is how Jim maintains his visibility.

Solve an Obvious Problem

"That's your entry point," says Jim. "You may want to transform how people think about their lives and the world, but you have to eat. Even if you want to think like a therapist, talk like a financial expert. Pick a popular topic, like quality, and by dint of that topic, you'll make a lot of relationships. You can expand from there.

"When I won the McKinsey Award, which is given annually to the best essay in the *Harvard Business Review*, a friend said, 'Put in an extra phone line.' I didn't have to do that, because no one called. My piece suggested one change one's frame of thinking: it was not an obvious piece about managing supply chains. A client reads a piece on a practical issue and says, 'Yes, I have that problem.' Then you sell a lot of work. It doesn't require the client to rethink his place in the world."

Take Your Relationships with You

"Understand that they are independent of your organisational situation," says Jim. "People can peel out of big companies and provide the function they were providing to those same companies. The organisation often likes it because they turn a fixed cost into a variable cost and they've got a better way to manage the deliverables."

There are big opportunities for those Jim calls "the glue people." "Companies used to have a set of Clark Clifford–like figures, young or old, who were extra to the organisation, who were trusted and trustworthy and could act to facilitate things. Now lean, macho organisations have dropped them. In the venture world there are a lot of those people, the venture capitalists

205

Great Work Finds You

are the glue people." Glue people are the ones with the names and numbers of others for whom they broker introductions mostly, or sometimes deals. Says Jim: "The guerilla warfare gangs, the solos, are out there getting all that business on their own. The glue people are outside the organisation providing that same function they used to provide on the inside."

Don't Overpromote Yourself

"You want to be like the great car mechanic that everybody refers their friends to."

Focus on what the other person's challenge is and how you can help them accomplish it.

"Do something differently and more effectively: There is a lot of value in that."

Build a Balanced Portfolio

"When I began consulting, the balance I needed was to work on some set of things I knew how to do, and some set of things I didn't have the foggiest idea how to do. The client let me do them because he didn't know anyone else who knew how to do them either. If I had too many routine projects, I didn't grow and I also didn't add that much value. If you just do things you know how to do, you soon are worthless. Your heart goes out of the business. You need someone to act as your conscience, who says to you periodically, 'Aim higher.'

"On the other hand if you have only the dark-night-of-the-soul projects, you burn out and go crazy.

"My portfolio now has things in it that I couldn't afford to do earlier. Half of my time goes to non-profit work. A lot of my time is for my wife and my kids. I don't have anything in the mundane category at this point."

Act Quickly and Make Things Happen Fast

"The velocity of market creation is so high, there are real opportunities if you can string together an ensemble fast [to work on a project]. If you know smart people, and they trust you enough, they are willing to let you help them. Solos who want to pilot big slow changes have a rude awakening ahead of them."

Make Yourself Easy to Buy

"Let people know you are available, and not in a way that encumbers them. Create a simple way for people to buy your services so that they don't have to marry you to work with you. Ben Shapiro at Harvard used to advertise his availability. At the beginning of the year he'd send a letter out to his clients and contacts and say, 'I'm getting ready to schedule my consulting time for the next year at such and such an amount per day. I have forty days available. If you want some of these days, send me a note.'"

Jim says there are people whose knowledge he'd love to buy, if only he knew how to approach them and ask their fees. Web pages are a great way to make your availability known. Include on your site the range of your fees, as in: "Speeches start at $3,000 plus expenses." Ask people to send you an e-mail requesting information on your fees. That way you have their addresses for your mailing list.

But there are other ways to make yourself visible and buyable.

VIABLE, NOT JUST BUYABLE

Why should potential clients be interested in you once they know you exist? Because you add value. One of the first things I had to do was think about the value I added. I called myself a writer, but writers are a dime a dozen. I said I was a consultant, but that's like introducing yourself as the new bee in a hive. How do you deliver value when your work is standard?

Every company and every leader has a problem, and the most interesting problems are the ones they deny they have. When you write about it or speak about what's still unspeakable, you educate people; you make it less useful for them to deny their problem because they have found someone—you—to help them solve it. That's how you connect with the clients closest to your own desire. For me the almost unspeakable problem is the issue of legacy: what outlives a person. It's in this area of the ultimate reputation that I spend a lot of consulting and speaking time.

Have a passion and declare it. That's how you make visible your value-added.

In the corporate world, leisure is the absence of work. In the solo world, you are most at leisure when you are most intensely involved. The same as true of artists. *Artists put their intense involvement on display for interested parties.* Display your intensity, passion, point of view; and would-be clients take notice. Talk to people about it. Large groups are great audiences, but so are dinner companions. Get the word out about the things that interest you.

I know of one soloist who is fascinated by U.S. presidents. He has studied the careers of presidents and used his findings about life at the top to attract the interest of executing who shared his fascination for the highest office in the land. His passion drew others to the questions he was investigating.

His point of view became his distinctive turf. He solved an obvious problem—leadership—in a unique way.

He also gained visibility by being quoted in trade magazines like *Red Herring* and *Upside* that carry news of new media startups. These are excellent sources. In the Internet world, as opposed, say, to the world of medicine, few people have any certainty about anything, and clients will take notice of someone with interesting ideas or questions. Even if you have never worked in new media, your expertise could translate.

How to get quoted? Most magazines hold conferences. Attend these meetings as a paying guest and meet the editors. Befriend them. Offer suggestions for stories. Offer help in your area of expertise. Become a "glue person" for the editors' needs.

At the same time as you broadcast an interest, narrowcast it. I have found it helpful to develop two carefully tailored mailing lists, twenty-five people in each. One is a list of *experts* in a field—people whose knowledge you respect and aspire to. The other is a list of friends and fellow-travellers who appreciate you professionally and would be glad to hear from you. Send these people your papers and other items of interest periodically (three times a year–not so often as to annoy and not so infrequently as to risk being forgotten). Write a personal note to each: I hate people who include me in their orgy of mass e-mails. Staying in touch with friends and experts might lead them to quote you or even pass on to you overflow work they can't handle.

Get to know a potential client much the same way an actor auditions for a role. Consultants prospecting for work have been known to ask clients, "What's on your mind?" or "What can I help you with?" Doing this means the client sets the agenda; the work is not co-created. Tony Award-winning actress Linda Franz, who won the role of Willy Loman's wife in the celebrated Broadway revival of *Death of a Salesman*, writes a novel about the character she's determined to play. Before an audition, she imagines details of the landscape the character might have grown up in, the character's relationship to her parents, and her conversations with friends. That is how she comes to understand more than the superficial person, and gets down to a person's strengths and weaknesses. "Grasp the cause and nature of others' suffering in order to understand their motivations and their rages, and suspend all judgment of them," says Franz. You don't have to write a novel about a client you hope to attract. But if you think of that client as a character you can play, you get inside his mind and know what he wants and needs. That understanding of him becomes a powerful draw for his attention.

A shortcut method for this is the technique of The Five Whys. Take one aspect of a potential client's typical behaviour and ask, "Why does X do this? Why is he killing himself doing deals? Because he's ambitious? Why is he so ambitious? Because he always talks about time being short. Why does time seem limited to him? He once mentioned in passing that his father died at the age he is now. How would X feel about other ways of making a difference than this subtle form of killing himself—like creating a new business or a philanthropy, to make time seem immortal?" Etc. You understand a person better by these exercises than if you asked him, "What would be of help to you? What troubles you?" To those questions, you never get the right answer, you get a safe answer. You get the client telling you something he already has figured out or is already working to solve.

Never ask the question to which you really want an answer. People evade direct questions. It puts them on the defensive. Instead ask any other question, even about the weather. You will get the answer to the tough question in the answer to the softball. What's bothering a person and what they want help with most, always comes out. We're always projecting our emotional state onto simple subjects.

Have fun creating your unique voice, and others will have fun listening to you. Maybe you are the best accountant within a hundred miles and clients will find you simply because you've declared yourself open for business. But maybe you've dreamed of consulting to politicians on ethical investing. To connect with those clients, lecture or write an article about the new millionaires, or conduct a study of how leaders make investment blunders. A professor of economics recently decided to test the theory that movie stars are a good return on studio investment. Big stars like Meg Ryan command contracts of several million dollars, but the professor found that these salaries aren't commensurate with profits. His results were contrarian (the stand soloists often take), and now he is being wined and dined in Hollywood and offered lucrative contracts.

Why me? Ask people who hire you why they came to you. Know what your attraction is so that you can reinforce these qualities in yourself. Use the same language others use about you in talking about yourself to potential clients.

Become a one-person souk. Soloists make requests, lots of them, and respond to requests from others. It's a good morning if at the end of an hour I have e-mailed at least five requests for information, or ideas, or counsel. I also respond quickly to others' requests.

Asking questions of others and providing answers is important. When others respond, they usually offer up information in kind, which someone else I know may need. So I open for business in my one-woman souk. I buy and trade and "sell" information periodically throughout the day. That's how I keep myself in circulation. Perhaps my name comes up in conversations. Perhaps people quote me, or say, "I just heard the following from Harriet Rubin this morning." Don Norman said, "My most valuable skill is the 10,000 names in my Palm Pilot. I end up bringing people together."

On the non-virtual level, it's valuable to do the same

thing. Before traveling to a city, go through your Rolodex and find those people living in your destination. Call people in advance, saying you'll be in town, asking if they have time for a coffee, or if you could come by and say hello. You can't expect people to remember you for great assignments when you are not in their line of sight.

Give speeches. The word on the street is that it's good to give lectures for about a year, and then to quit. By then your name will have filtered up to others' attention.

PROPOSE!

Proposals are documents that invite a potential client to co-create something with you. I evaluated proposals every day as a publisher; now I'm writing them. I've seen enough of them to know that the signal success of a proposal is strutting out what you know, but even more, it is in describing what you don't know. The most exciting part of any proposal comes in the questions you raise, in describing the search to be made.

A proposal can be brief, from two to five pages, and should cover five basic sections:

1. The question/problem, summarised and high-lighted up front.

2. The problem, contextualised—offer the social, cultural, or trend-related reasons that the question has

214

come up for the client; the client shouldn't feel he's saddled with an unusual problem. He should feel instead that he is among the first to have discovered the problem.

3. Sources to give the questions heft and weight and interest.

4. Description of the nature of the study you will conduct: how long it will last, what resources you will draw on.

5. Your qualifications.

Think in terms of conflict, namely a question that needs to be solved. Write as if you are having fun. In fact, have fun! Use your real voice, not some zombified professional voice. Write everything as if you are writing a murder mystery: A reader should not remember blinking; that's how thrilling the material should be and can be if you open with the question and spellbind the reader with how you will solve it technically and imaginatively.

A few tricks: Use almost no adjectives or adverbs. Mix short sentences and long ones, close-ups of the problem and long views of trends. Best-selling novelist James Ellroy said that just when he thinks he's finished, he goes back over the manuscript and takes out half the words. Most are throat-clearing noises, and if you eliminate them, you keep your reader immersed.

Here's how I made a proposal to one client, using many of the approaches addressed throughout this chapter. I met her on a "blind date" when a mutual friend sent her a copy of my book.

Nina Brink, forty-five-year-old dynamo founder/ CEO of World On Line, Europe's AOL, had read *The Princessa* and wanted to meet me. There was no agenda, just hello, and laughter and trading stories over a quick muffin. I had a great time with her. But I was very surprised when she called a few days later and asked if I would write a book about her company. The subject of working together never came up during our meeting. I thought about the old days as a publisher when I chased business like a bwana on the big hunt. The soloing trip certainly is different: Don't seek; ye shall be found. I told Nina that I would think about her offer.

I considered Nina's offer, but with little enthusiasm. Writing someone else's book seemed too much like my old publishing life. And I am no longer a servant to others; I'm free. So I responded with a counter-offer. I changed Nina's proposal into a proposal of my own.

I retrieved a report I'd filed showing that 85 percent of financial analysts bought shares of a company because of the chief executive's reputation. I used this argument in my formal proposal to Nina. I quoted the study, which said: "Celebrity bosses help distinguish their companies from their rivals by giving them a human face. And they can use their store of respect to help dig their companies out of a crisis. The companies run by the top ten most-admired bosses recovered almost four times faster from the recent market correction than those run by the least-admired ones."

Here's the learning-a-living angle: I proposed to do for Nina what I am trying to do for myself. Maybe I will learn how to craft my new identity by crafting Nina's. And perhaps, by understanding what Nina has built, I can learn how she is shaping her legacy. I wrote the following proposal. For the purpose of this book, I annotate the strategy behind each paragraph.

> *Dear Nina,*
>
> *Strategically it would be of great value for your company to have a book published about your practice and ideas. Studies show the investment value of companies rises when they become "celebrity companies." In the attention economy, being noticed is everything.*
>
> [The opening paragraph puts the value-added proposition, up front. But the next paragraph introduces a conflict, a tension, and sets up the need for a solution.]
>
> *The challenge is that the business book market is saturated. The critical factor in a having a book accepted for publication is in the angle or the "pitch."*

A straightforward story about WOL or Earthlink or Exxon for that matter would not be enough to interest a publisher. But if there is a publishable story to be found, I will find it and give you the means to get a book published.

[That is a statement of the obstacle and the promise, both.]

The project would have two phases. First: I would spend a full day interviewing you and a second day interviewing the top officers of your company, preferably on site in Holland. From what I learn in these meetings, I would write and submit to you a report outlining a book proposal, focusing on WOL's ideas, practices, and vision of the future—and what makes you unique in these areas. This outline would express what is timeless about your company, and what is timely and newsworthy. The first will be important to book publishers, the other will bring you to the attention of the business press, which will raise WOL's profile.

[This letter is an upside-down pyramid: the big picture yielding to the more specific details and promises. In this paragraph just above, the promise is described in detail, and in terms of process. I'm guiding Nina's questions and focusing on the process as the means to address them. It is that, more than the solutions, that

will capture a reader's interest. The client
begins to see herself inside the drama, where
your interests connect.]

*The second phase of the project is to put you in
contact with writers and agents who would develop a
finished proposal from the outline and then market
the book to publishers. If I can accomplish this with a
few phone calls, no additional fee is billed. If, however,
it becomes necessary to attend meetings with you and
interested publishers, I would bill you at my daily rate.*

[Dividing the project into two phases gives
the client a sense of what she could build up to,
if she cares. And a sense that she is playing it
relatively safe by choosing the first option only.]

*I have done this work for the last ten years for
several top American CEOs and consultants. I
routinely approached them with ideas for books. I
developed outlines for them, and matched them with
writers. For many, the returns were significant. My
author Max De Pree, then CEO of Herman Miller, was
reborn as a statesman with a world-class reputation
when his book,* Leadership Is an Art, *was published.
Peter Senge rose from obscurity as a part-time lecturer
into an internationally recognised management guru
after I worked with him to develop* The Fifth
Discipline. *Observers have said that Andy Grove's
book,* Only the Paranoid Survive, *contributed to*

his winning Time's *Man of the Year award. Grove's*
book helped establish him as a Kissinger of business
at a time when the perception of him was someone
who made a product no one could explain, in an
industry few understood.

[Put yourself in context. Tell who you are
and what you have done. Don't be shy but
don't hype yourself. Be matter-of-fact.]

Please understand that I cannot guarantee a
successful publication. But my track record in this
area is very strong.

[A caveat, if appropriate, signals that you are
aware of all possibilities, including failure. It
also puts the client subliminally on notice that
you can't do it alone; her involvement is vital.]

Although technically this is work of the kind I'd
sworn I'd never do again, there were now eighteen
months separating me and Doubleday. I can appreciate
my old skills without being afraid they will hold me
hostage to the past. Reinventing Nina's offer into my
own makes all the difference. Change the conditions of
the work, and the work itself changes. When you're in
control, any work is beautiful.

Nina phoned two weeks later to say she liked my
proposal. She was confident she would get the approval
of her board to pursue it.

HOW TO CHARGE

"The world of consultants is mired in secrecy," says Don Norman. When he went solo this year he found that "one of the biggest mysteries is how to charge. Tom Peters gave me some guidelines. He said, 'Keep raising your rates. When people start rejecting you, that's when you've reached the correct rate for you.'"

Consultant Allan Kennedy suggests that £300 an hour or between £3,000 and £6,000 a day plus expenses is a good amount for someone on the middle to high end of the competency and reputation scale.

There are dozens of other ways to charge for your knowledge and your learning. You will have a lot of clients in whom you are making an investment of time working on a project whose payback is significant learning. Charging clients is no simple matter. For additional and more daring payment models, see the chapter "Love Like You've Never Been Hurt, Dance Like Nobody's Watching, and Work Like You Don't Need the Money."

WHEN TO FIRE A CLIENT

I had to fire my first client recently. I joined his advisory board to co-create a leadership institute. But the closer the client got to his ideal, the more he started to pull back on his bold plans. Staying on the board would have limited my own imagination, and it could have harmed my reputation to be associated with a project where the level of risk and daring is so small. I resigned. I'd never said goodbye to any legitimate job before. It was like burying a beloved pet.

It's very scary, when you have few assignments and are just starting out, to even think of firing a client. But doing so makes room for other clients to find you.

A SAMPLE CLIENT PORTFOLIO

On the following page is my client portfolio, which strives for diversity and balance.

In this list, I mention only the ongoing relationships, not the one-shots. In each case, I didn't solicit the business. Most of these relationships had the gestation cycle of a dinosaur, a decade being the longest, the shortest being two weeks from meeting to deal. The average time from hello to bread on the table was three years.

In learning my living, I want to serve my clients and deepen my craft of communications. The challenge or study I've set myself is this: People talk of continuous improvement in service or manufacturing or quality; why not in leaders? My clientele is the perfect "open university" for that goal. Interestingly, all but one of these clients is a company that didn't exist five years ago.

Only two clients are paying my Allan Kennedy–inspired daily fee. Otherwise I work below fee and in one case merely for an honorarium because the opportunity to learn and build my brand is significant.

Client	How the Client Found Me	What I'm Doing for the Client/ and Learning in Return
Nina Brink, WOL	My book	Identity development/Insights into leadership
Website	My book	Online leadership seminars/Crash course in the new media
P.B.	Met at a conference	Developing a book project/How to get on TV and national radio
Zine Zone	Through Avram	Serving on the board of one of the companies/ Learning how boards work
Fast Co.	Friendship	Writing, serving as consulting editor/Building my brand, learning to tell stories about the new economy
Radio show	By shifting a different request	Contributing book stories/Learning to write scripts, build an oral storytelling voice

My portfolio is a fair mix. I have one big company, WOL, which is an important and a distinguishing feature in any soloist's portfolio. I have a new media company and a traditional media company—a publisher. Varying the size of clients is good, and paying attention to how many are in the old world of service or manufacturing businesses vs. the highly entrepreneurial world of information businesses is also important. A strong portfolio is one where if all the companies were to gather in a room, it would turn into a great party. But for someone who claims strategy and leadership as her bailiwick, I am missing a representation in politics.

What is your portfolio? Write out a list of your clients—real and ideal—according to the categories of size, creativity, freedom, action, and others. Give yourself points for learning and balance.

Letting work find you is an ambitious endeavour. It is also scary to wait for opportunities to attract you. But it is the way to get great clients in the new world of soloing.

14. Serving the Higher Voice

Now that you're solo, you can take the biggest risk of all: acting on the belief that you have something unique to offer the world. You do. The nature of solo assignments reinforces that belief into a reality.

Solo work is not solely about expediency, quality, or efficiency. It is creating something you could not have fathomed at the start. It is about discovery, surprise, and unevenness. It is about the higher version of quality, which is not consistency, or sameness but which is art whose goal cannot be known at the outset, because it always involves a transformation, a surprise. Solo work brings out of the soloist far more than he could have expected.

To a great gardener, a bouquet has to be of ikebana quality, where each flower is a placed as if it were drawn onto a canvas: with deliberateness, not expediency. When you work with a client or on intellectual property, you can achieve the level of art. But only if you appeal to the client's highest motives. This is not always easy, considering that a business relationship is also practical. But it is possible. Solo consulting can approach an art if both you and the client create a relationship that goes beyond the aims either of you could have stated at the start. It's up to you to get it to that height.

How you reach this point consistently in client work is by serving the higher voice. That is the voice each of you has when you are free of daily concerns and nagging personal stresses, and when fears or time pressures or financial worries don't get in the way. When you constantly remember this higher voice, learn to listen for it, respect it when you hear it, it acts as your compass. When you hear it in clients, you will hear it in yourself. It is the voice of your ideals: your work uncompromised. You can afford to yield to it, now that you are a solo. You can afford to serve it.

The goal is for each of you not just to learn something about the task at hand for which you were hired, but to have a mutual impact. It's the difference between *teaching* someone and *touching* someone deeply.

Consultant Jim Moore said he had this kind of shaping relationship early in his career with one of his first clients, Muppet creator Jim Henson. Jim Moore learned from Henson how to develop his own unique voice. "Henson always had this belief that being a creative person is a bit like being a turtle without your shell. You have to put a lot of yourself out there, and even if you are Jim Henson, not everything you do will work.

"On the other hand, if you don't put your joy and your personality and what inspires you forward, then you don't really have anything unique out there at all. And that is a fairly terrible place to be . . . as a person and as a solo."

Serve a client's ideals as a way to solve his immediate problem. That's how you develop your own higher voice, your own unique skills that you need to do as a solo to compete with others and with big, full-service companies. As a solo, you can develop the courage to express your vision and live it out, like a naked turtle.

How can you and a client work together in such a way that you can realise the opportunity to do more than the job at hand? How can a soloist go beyond the typical client-expert relationship, which is possible because a solo has no one to report back to? Think of this as a double helix: The more you serve the higher voice, the more the client is likely to match your intensity and vision. Remember: You're the boss, even though it's the client who pays the bills. You can, if you are to learn your living, take a risk with each relationship. You must, if you are to realise the solo's great pleasure in work: making an art of your work.

Jim Moore recounts the process by which this can be done. He speaks from the point of view of a consultant, but his ideas about serving the higher voice have meaning for a solo in any relationship.

LISTEN FOR MULTIPLE VOICES

"The client's agenda comes first," says Jim. "That's the essence of a client relationship. This means being totally devoted to the other person's agenda, and to serving the higher voice of that person, building enough intimacy so that when that person slips from their higher agenda—when that person either loses confidence or becomes self-centred or becomes deluded—then at those moments you can say, 'Hey, I thought this was about the goal you have that is really courageous.'

"Clients have multiple voices—the result of multiple demands on them." Some are practical, some expedient, and some counter to their own good. "You try to have a relationship with their highest self. They become confident of that, and they know that when they walk away from that encounter with you, they will be reinforced in acting at their highest level.

"You have to be on the side of telling the truth, facing the bad stuff as well as the good stuff. I have a hand-written notice hanging in my office that says, 'Truth Is Our Friend.' That comes up for discussion a lot in client meetings. Part of what one has to do is set up the expectation that there will be things we won't want to face, and part of the way we support each other is to face those things in a constructive way, not avoid them, and not be overwhelmed by them.

"You have to be able to inject energy. In the moments when the other person finds their agenda overwhelming or their world view caving in, you have to remind the client that this is what they set out to do."

RESPECT THE LOGIC OF SUCCESS

To attain the higher voice, a solo needs to learn what makes the client uniquely successful. A solo respects "the logic of success" and at the same time doesn't get overwhelmed by it.

"'Physician do no harm,'" says Jim. "Your ability to help another person will be determined by your ability to understand the subtle dimensions of what is working for the person, or what could work for him.

"Not-so-hot consultants are sorely limited by their notion of what it is to have a successful system. They have primitive models. The good ones are very sophisticated about understanding the success logic and tweak

229

and poke it or even restructure it. They understand what is working in a social system. There are always multiple aspects: social, financial, managerial, spiritual. The essence of a client relationship is understanding what is working and what may be uniquely working."

Appreciate what your client has achieved. Help him develop this, whatever may be the problem you are hired on to solve. Keep working for that highest ability of the client's. But also be careful that you don't let what your client does best overwhelm you.

"When I first got hired by Jim Henson," says Moore, "the screenwriter Michael Borman, whose credits include *The Good Mother*, gave me some advice about working with powerful people. He said, 'A guy like Henson can probably count on the fingers of one hand the people who are honest with him. Everyone else is somehow trying to hustle him out of something. You have the opportunity to be one of the honest people. You've got to watch out not to get swept up into the other group, because Henson will know right away.'

"Borman was right. As soon as you get swept in, you lose your higher voice. A new consultant can see a client who is wealthy or powerful [or wealthier and more powerful than himself], and know that person could help you in a minute. You can't get swept away, because once you do, you're in that dance, and you know you're bullshitting.

"That's the whole essence of spiritual disciplines. It's about being centred and taking a deep breath and looking into your heart. That's not to say that you just blurt out what you see. The other issue in a client relationship is that there are moments when you are building rapport and there are moments when you are making interpretations. There are times when you are doing 'strategic pandering' and there are times when you are confronting.

"You want to know when you are pandering in the service of truth and seeing issues confronted. There are times when you have false clarity, particularly when you are entering into a relationship with a client." False clarity is thinking you know the client's problems. Or thinking you can address them with an off-the-shelf solution.

"That's why it's important to know the logic of success that exists in anybody who is successful. Other people viewing a leader's situation could see in one day's analysis what the business problems were. In Jim Henson's case, it was that he wasn't a good manager. But he wasn't supposed to be a good manager. David Lazer, Henson's alter ego, said: 'Jim Henson is this kind of Jungian hero who comes across once in a generation.' David's view was that leaders like Jim are extraordinarily rare and of course they have issues. But on the other hand they can do things no one else can do. If you have the opportunity, you serve them, because that is a rare moment.

"When Henson died, the rector Paul Moore said in his eulogy, in essence, 'I'm envious of this guy because *he managed to make good fun*.' There was a sense of regret, that 'I can't do that. I'm always making good sound should.'"

"This whole idea about the higher voice," says Jim Moore, "is the idea of 'satyagraha.'" This is the term Mahatma Gandhi coined for his belief that not just a resolution but a higher state could be achieved out of any conflict if the people involved could find a single larger agenda that they cocreated. "Jim was doing satyagraha, not in a micro way" or one-to-one, "but in a macro way" in the work, in building his vision. "Jim kept building a consistent voice. He made great movies, but he also made bad and stupid movies. His film *Labyrinth* was a midlife crisis lived out in celluloid. But creatively he was a loving presence." The higher voice is served by experimentation. Following up on lots of ideas, especially the silly ones, deepens one's faith in one's creative process.

"Jim would stay close to love," says Moore. The Muppet Mansion—the Manhattan headquarters—was this evidence of this love writ large. The excitement inside was palpable. You'd walk in the door but you'd really be walking into Henson's mind and spirit. Puppets would

232
Soloing

be suspended from the ceiling. Stuffed Kermits filled the shelves. There was a Muppet workshop in the mansion until the fumes from the glue got to be too much. Henson's vision left its mark on everything. His love was expressed through his imagination.

A COMPANY IN WHICH BEING SOLO IS NOT BEING ALONE

Helping a leader leverage the qualities which make him unique keeps him in the soloist's camp. Leaders who are uncompromising are often flying solo in that they have no peers.

That is how Jim Moore learned a lot about soloing from Jim Henson. "What I learned from Jim was how to build an enterprise around your own vision. In a way he consulted to me without knowing it. Jim was the first person I knew who built an enterprise around making his own vision happen in the world. Henson Associates was a personal platform company and a multi-dimensional one," says Moore. "The movies periodically made a lot of money, but in order to make those successful, you needed to build relationships, and that could be done through the Muppet books, the deals with Children's Television Workshop, and the Muppet shows. He built multiple relationships with audiences at multiple levels."

The Muppet monopoly was essentially a solo effort,

233

sustained by employees who were invited in to learn, but not invited to share in the vision as equals or partners. In today's businesses, equity is becoming a norm. But Henson followed the opposite approach. He was a generous but private person and very much a loner where his vision was concerned.

"I learned a lot about the control of a personal business. I was tempted from time to time to build a business with partners who would be my equals. But Jim gave out no equity in his business, just profit participation. Jim learned how to give out various kinds of economic rights but keep the creative rights and then not have to fight over them with anybody. Jim could therefore really develop his own vision.

"Jim was betting on his vision. If your vision was different, he believed you should go and build your own organisation. He didn't want partners fighting with him about what his vision should be. That would be a waste for everybody. If you were working for Jim, you were working on his agenda. He was the only person identified as 'creator.' That was his title. Jim never allowed any understudies."

The logic of success here was not trying to turn Jim Henson into a team or into a systems institution like GE. Says Jim Moore: "Part of how I consult is to analyse what is happening: understanding implicit structures to make them explicit, and then show people how they work. My job was not to change Jim Henson into every other Hollywood producer but to help what could happen there happen. Moore's job, as he saw it, was to make Henson a better soloist inside an organisation.

"At a certain point you say to the world, 'I'm going to rise or fall on my vision.' I learned that from Henson."

It's not just archetypal figures like Henson who have a higher voice. All of us who solo have it. Says Moore: "What we're all trying to do as consultants is support each other's higher voices.

"It's all one big friends meeting, trying to find each other's higher voice and help each other with our limitations."

15. Thoreau.com

There is one place a single-minded soloist can be as powerful as any monster brand, and that is on the Web. "In the cloud," Avram calls the Web, a soloist can have no money yet have a presence, a Web face, that attracts clients, resources, and capital. In the way a logo used to define a brand identity, a Website does now. Web faces speak a whole different language of identity from the old version of identity building: those antique trappings known as the logo and the company name.

My biggest fear on being orphaned from Doubleday was the loss of identity. I rushed to a designer who had experience in creating corporate identities. I came up with a clever name,

Rubicon, that combined my interest in leadership with my brand-promise: to help leaders cross a difficult passage in their professional lives and emerge stronger and wiser, same as the great Caesar who crossed a river, the Rubicon, and changed his and history's destiny. I liked the pun of "Rubin," my surname, and the abbreviation, inserted, of "co." for "company" in Rubicon. My designer charged a Caesar's ransom and devised a logo, a letterhead, a business card, a mailing label—the logo was a blue globe with a red line—for the red river— running through it. "This is it," I thought, "my own turf." The big boys have logos; now *I* had a logo. The big boys had a name, now *I* had a name. So what if I was some lost soul, wandering the plains without a big corporate identity, a ronin, one of those masterless samurai whose master had died and should have committed seppuku to end the clan. In ancient Japan, a samurai without his master was no one. Who was I without my master company? Someone! The logo proved it.

But I could never push the button and start the presses rolling on the letterhead and cards. "What do you need another name for?" Avram asked. "It's hard enough to brand one name, your own, why try to brand two?" Not only that, the extra name seemed fake. I had freed my soul from the corporation to be me. Why suddenly don another mask? Out of insecurity? Out of trying to be like Them?

237

Thoreau.com

I pulled the plug on the logo project and sought my identity elsewhere—on the other side of the mirror where whole new concepts of identity prevail—concepts that favour the soloist. Identity building used to be about repetition and stability. Campbell's soup repeats its red-on-white logo ad nauseam. Intel slaps its Pentium logo on everything. Organisations are very good at this form of identity building, and when you get free of them, it is natural to think in corporate terms to extend your brand identity into the market. But solo identities play by a different set of rules.

If Thoreau were alive today, he might have set up Walden on the Net and not bothered with the mud and the rain and the beans of the pond. Walden would be Thoreau.com.

One quick clarification. A brand is not an identity. A brand is a promise (see the chapter "Brand-New You"). Identity is the face on the promise: a swoosh, or mouse ears. Brand vs. identity is like the difference between a person and a personality. A person (brand) is male/female, white/dark-skinned, etc. Relatively unchangeable. A personality (identity) is mood: happy/gloomy, stingy/ generous: totally changeable. While your brand won't change, your identity will change often in the new world of selling and marketing. Change is the hallmark of the new identity. To some degree or other, change will be a key element in devising your identity on the Web.

You need an identity. The best soloists are hypersensitive to style. They pay it exquisite attention. Style carries through their products and their behavior. Macintosh computers sell because they don't look like your standard PCs. That sense of differentness is driven throughout the company by Steve Jobs, who in Apple's early years would run through the parking lot to study the design of the cars, from the rounded lines of the Mercedes to the toy-box look of the Porsches. He'd copy elements he loved onto the casings of his computers to give each generation of computers its own distinctive look. It had a powerful effect in creating Apple's identity—and Jobs's as a wizard with technology. Apple customers used to say that if they cut themselves, they'd bleed in all the colours of the Apple logo.

SOLO IS NOT A CORPORATE IDENTITY DIVIDED BY 1, 10, 100, OR 1,000

A solo identity is not, therefore, a big company identity writ small. It is another creature entirely. Memorable solo identities are built out of these two elements:

- Constancy
- AND change.

Your brand (promise) won't change. But your identity should. "It's like Lego," says Thomas Mueller, creative director of Razorfish, the hot digital identity company. Your brand is you; it doesn't change. That's the part that's constant in building an identity. Your identity, on the other hand, can reflect various styles. "Here is a helpful way to think of how these two get combined: However you put Lego together—into a skyscraper, a tree, a wall—in the end, it's still Lego."

The whole world is changing constantly, so identities must change too. This is especially true for soloists, who play many different roles to many different constituencies. A great leader like George Washington said, "Character is a character you play again and again." But not in the twentieth century. I am the carrier of one message to my audiences, the carrier of another to my executive clients, yet another to the public for business ideas. For the soloist, conventional notions of identity can become a trap. "Every time work could have become my identity, I walked away," said Bill Drenttel. He left the ad business and has one foot out the door of the design business. He is now not only redesigning the Netscape browser, he's also publishing books and working as the architect of his home and office. He's one person, but he's not trapped inside the prison of a monolithic identity.

True identity is whatever is true at the moment. The medium for expressing your varied identity is the Web, where you can and should change your moods or facets of your identity every day.

FINDING LIFE IN THE WEBSITE UNIVERSE

Take advantage of how much stature and contact you can have on the Web. Don't build one Website. Build two: a personal/professional site and a business site.

A business Website has several advantages.

- It describes your up-to-the-minute professional expertise and expands it into an independent service or source of information.
- It provides the opportunity to engage in e-commerce, selling or trading your expertise or books or gadgets you favour, continually amending the list.
- It serves as the billboard for advertising if you choose to solicit it, which will vary as editorial copy varies.
- It provides a network in which visitors to the site can share ongoing questions and information, thus developing a loyalty to you.

A Website allows you to shift in and out of new identities. I thought I was Harriet Rubin until Avram said, "Let's do a Website called TheSoloist.com." In that instant, I became a Web face for a new satellite business called www.ivillage.com/TheSoloist. To build a site that generates revenue and clients is important in extending your identity.

To promote a site, talk it up, e-mail friends inviting

them to log on, visit local radio stations to promote it whenever you travel, generate cross links to other people's sites, all to build eyeballs. Take out classified ads in newspapers advertising your site. These are cheap. Put the site on your business card. And if possible, attach yourself to an already established vertical site. It's easy to find these: Go to one of the search engines, like Yahoo. Type in keywords that identify you, and then see what similar sites are found. Contact the Web masters to establish a cross-link. If your site is already well-established, contact the business development manager at the bigger sites and propose a joint venture.

If you generate enough popularity for your business site, you not only build a loyal client base for yourself, you might be able to sell your site to a buyer who needs content.

My first stop was www.oznic.com to register the site name. I made sure the name was not already claimed. I paid the fee and in twenty-four hours had claim to my domain, my storefront on the Web. A good site name is like a headline in advertising. It should be as simple as possible and point to you or your service. It's becoming more important to reserve your domain name today than it is to incorporate.

Next I started a folder of ideas for the content. I decided to follow the standard magazine format and include features and secondary articles, and think of changing the "cover" or major story every month at least to keep the site fresh and bank on the elements of change. I also decided to keep the text short under each header. Flash card format is how people absorb information on the Web. Here is what I came up with to develop my interests into Web-worthy content.

- *Cover story.* Monthly featured interviews with soloists as varied as a brilliant street magician, a one-man skunk works, who is one of the legion of self-employed inventors who have given the economy everything from wings to water beds; or the winner of this year's Iditarod (an epic dog-sled race), who works with eighty-six Alaskan huskies but otherwise alone.
- *A column on tools.* Regular updates on the best insurance packages, the design of solo workspaces, the best money manager, time management system, etc.
- *E-commerce opportunities.* The site will sell items soloists have found to make their lives easier: everything from digital recorders to newsletters.
- *Makeunders.* Accounts of people who reinvent themselves from corporado to soloist, shedding the trappings of corporate life.
- *Secrets of the trade.* How great soloists gain an edge.
- *Networking.* How to find people to talk to and to trade goods and services.

And so on. The details on my site are offered as an example of how to take a one-person business and make it into a profitable venture. In creating this site, I'm keeping my soloist purity. I am designing content for the site but I'm NOT an employee of the company called The Soloist. I am working as a consultant to the site and holding equity. I did this by finding a partner to manage the site and handle the financing, the design, and the site maintenance.

Once I had created sample content, I set about finding a designer to create the homepage. This is a critical feature of any site, just as a magazine cover sells a magazine. A homepage is the front page. It should be simple. Ease of use is everything. If the site is difficult to use, people will click away quickly. It also needs to be visually interesting, emphasising images more than words.

People need to develop a loyal emotional relationship to your site. It's useful to study how Apple built that up for its product line. Macintosh people are so intensely loyal that they wait longer than they should for an updated machine. They try to convince others there is nothing better. Nobody does that with Intel. Imagine if people felt about you and your work the way they feel about Apple.

They might, if you give viewers who come to your site an emotional experience. Websites should create the opportunity to change a person's life. They should give a person the chance to adopt a new set of friends, or obtain new knowledge. As one consultant advised me, "If you come to a site and find a solution to a problem you have *and* get laid, you're a customer for life."

THE PERSONAL SITE

www.ivillage.com/TheSoloist is a business site. My personal site is a reflection of me, and like me, most of it has to do with my work, but also with my passion for art and books and poetry. Even though the focus is on me, the site emphasises my work. I depend on it to create a community of people interested in the same professional issues as I am on leadership and story-telling. I also use it to inform clients about the person who stands behind her work.

A personal site is important for these reasons:

- People get to know who you are.

On my Harriet Rubin site, I reprint my published articles (or links to the sites that have them), and radio stories, including notes on how and why I did the stories done and offering information about the stories in progress. This gives viewers a forum for seeing how I wrestle with problems and opportunities of telling stories and developing themes that they might find useful. And it offers a place to exchange ideas for crafting nonfiction stories. I will also include background on me, even baby pictures. People tend to be interested in how a person achieved success or even failure, over a lifetime and in the course of a single project. They want to know more about a person whose work interests them.

- You also have an opportunity to give things back to the community.

A personal website can provide a great service by telling people how you got through an illness, say, or a divorce or a firing or some other crisis.

My personal site contains information friends or other writers may want to know about me—but not my clients. On my business site, I offer specific information and engage in e-commerce. I will link viewers back and forth between the two sites.

A designer friend offered to create my personal site. He began by asking me what I want my website to offer to potential clients and readers:

1. The text of articles I've written (or any papers, commentaries, etc.).

2. A narrative I will write to link articles so readers can track the bigger themes.

3. Notes and paragraphs that were edited out of the published stories, including perhaps the response the

stories provoked, for readers who want to follow up with sources or dig deeper into subject matter I've covered. ("Personal" material like pages from your diary would also work.)

4. A continually updated booklist of good reading and pointers to an online bookseller so readers can locate the books (or any list of favourites: movies, meals, etc.).

5. Pictures and photos, to give the site a casual scrapbook feeling.

6. A bimonthly column I'd write just for the site.

7. Notes on writing and selling non-fiction (or how you do what you do).

And I mention the two most important requirements:

8. A means to maintain the site myself (to save on monthly maintenance charges).

9. Built-in multiple secret passageways so I can preview my new book and research for selected readers.

In our planning session, John, the designer, sat opposite me in a deep slouch. To provoke any reaction, I asked how we go about creating the site. He said that if he was inspired by something he heard from me, he would get up and start mapping on the whiteboard. He stayed very still.

He started by asking these questions:

What are your favourite colours? Or is everything various shades of black for you?

No, I say, I love the entire palette, but in the vivid range: barn red, vivid green, deep blue.

Do you know an oak leaf when you see one?

Yes.

How about poison ivy?

Yes.

Would you know timothy?

Who? I say.

Where were you born?

Passaic.

What is it?

A town in northern New Jersey that industry forgot.

How long did you live there?

Eighteen years, until I found out there was no lock on the door at home.

Did you launder your tennis sneakers in your twenties?

No.

You wore them scuffed?

No, I wore jogging shoes, and nobody washes them.

Oh, so you were rich enough to have specialised sports shoes?

No, all I had was a pair of jogging shoes.

What did you play tennis in?

I never played tennis. (I am beginning to feel like Kato Kaelin. No, Mr. Darden, those weren't my unwashed tennies under the bed.)

So, you wore jogging shoes? Did you like them scuffed?

Yes! I scream. (Is John a rubber shoe fetishist?)

This is what passes for psychoanalysis in WebWorld. Don't be put off by it. This is how your identity is translated out of you in bits and bytes and images. By asking these questions, John is trying to find out the colours, symbols, "look and feel" of my personality. Am I a nature girl, sports-minded, rich or poor in heritage? His questions are designed to frame a context for my site.

Okay, I know enough, John said and jumped up. He suddenly found himself a backbone. He reached for the whiteboard.

"I know what your website should look like," he said: "a plant. At the roots will be you, your identity. At the top, the plant will flower with articles you are writing, and the books you are developing. Most plants aren't vertical, they grow in many directions at once. So will yours.

"Let's run the site backward," John said, "and see it as

249

a person would use it. If a magazine reader likes your article, he might try to imagine, 'What's she like? What was she as a kid? Is she some woman who's angry and had a bad marriage? Has she had an easy go of things?' That's what people will want to know. They'll want to know you.

"What do you want people to say about your site after they've been there?" John asks.

"I want them to say they learned something new—a new way of thinking about their lives. They might tell me what they'd wished they'd seen in a story. Or have tips for other stories. I want to take people with me as I head into the frontiers of business and report back on the people at the edge doing the latest, greatest, and most dangerous things."

Okay, says John. Here's the Website conceptually. It's personal and professional. At the highest level, it shows the visitor: Here are my views. That's the flower. The stem is: Here's where I came from. Here's where I picked up my ideas. Then the roots: your childhood, high school, college. Get comments from your teachers, if you can, or a few of your pals. Photos of them would be great. I want you to get quotes from Gladys Clutterbuck who says, "I always knew she'd get into trouble."

Weeks later, John has a prototype for me to see. I walk in and see a long-stemmed flower, very giraffelike and delicate. There is a neat little bulb at the bottom, my name in lilac, and these clickable categories: Background, Thoughts, Printed Material.

My heart sinks. Way too girly, I think, and way too static. A plant is rooted. The minute I see it I realise it's the opposite of me. I'm not delicate. I'm not rooted. A Web designer friend said he'd imagined me symbolised more as an arc, suggesting movement, a launch into space and a descent to Earth with a story.

"I have trouble with that," John said about the arc when I mention it. "An arc is too mathematically precise. Your life has been one of being open to chance and making intuitive leaps. You stand for something people have to know about themselves. Which is that you came from a humble background and made something of yourself. You stand for the fact that we think all wrong about success in this culture. Success is random, it's being open to chance. Men have known this all along and when a job offer comes up that takes them to Venezuela, they go. But most people think success is preordained. It isn't. You're more like lightning. I'd even suggest you call your site Lucky Strike. The theme is 'open to change' vs. 'not open to change.'"

We compromise and create a timeline that is like an arc. It moves on cyclical time, not dates but recurring events——cycles——like the start of a project, its development and completion. Included as background are

251

diary pages. John plans to embed in it audio clues. Opening a diary will have one sound—maybe the snap of a binding opening up—and turning the pages will have another sound. We wonder if it is possible to add the sound of an eraser going eee-eeck—ee, screaming across the "page," trying to take out something really hot. Audio cues are an uncharted area of the web design. "They are going to be a huge business," John says.

HOW MUCH OF YOU SHOULD BE ON DISPLAY?

Avram's site is much more personal than my own. Although he also designed a professional website, this personal site is meant primarily for his large network of friends and acquaintances who know him through his music, his public service, and his struggle against prostate cancer.

Avram has become a crusader against prostate cancer, and at the same time he is building a house in the wine country of California. He wants to share the benefits of what he's learned in these pursuits. Cancer has called him to use every investigative and negotiating skill he developed in thirty years of business. But it was the cancer that taught him how to build a life outside of work. Building a house is part of that effort to start a new life. For those who find themselves in similar situations, his site contains information about his diet and medical odyssey, about health, prevention, and detection. Click on the image of his house and up come blueprints and other lessons in building. There is a level of information on the site that is very personal, and only chosen friends are given the password to enter those areas.

Most of the work of creating the site went into the building of the front page. For a month, he and his Web designer Jerry Brown asked themselves: What defines a life?

"The things that struck me about Avram's identity," said Jerry, "is the seriousness with which he thinks of his cancer and the beauty of the house he's building. Art came into it. I wanted to know about his tastes in art. Does he get up full of energy or linger and weave into the day? How does he strike people? How does he act in groups? What first impression does he make on others? I need to know that to know how the page will strike people. It's his identity, after all. What Web designers are creating is communication. I want to know what and how Avram himself communicates.

"A web page is a stage and a designer's job is to create what takes place there.

"I try to figure out a way to create a contrast, to give an illusion of depth with one quick flash. One client, formerly a record producer, now a soloist, wanted to make an impression of a powerful Hollywood famous person. The site could be repulsive and ego-driven if it weren't handled delicately. My job is to make it playful. I use contrasts to build suspense and surprise and draw viewers in. I chose a very pastel, gradient palette to contrast with the heavy hype in the text."

Since Web pages' first impressions are made in a burst of light, Jerry concentrates on colours "to create the identity." Avram's site uses cool early morning colours, mostly the grey-blues of ocean and sky. "The opening page will contain more than one image. Avram wants people to go to the site to find out about cancer, the house, and his public service work. It is not a self-serving site.

"People are afraid to reveal themselves, they want to be a little bit disguised. They often have no control over who visits their site. There is a growing demand for protected sites. Most people want to create an alter ego, an image of the way they want to be and be seen. I would prefer to reveal people as they are. Because there is always something interesting about them. Revealing sites can be the most alluring. *That's when a person gives something back*, when they said: 'This is something I've learned, this is my struggle.'

"Sites have got to become hotter and more personal, but not only through text. The graphic artist has to figure out a way to create warmth symbolically, to create it through colour, movement, to suggest it, to suggest warmth."

CHOOSING A DESIGNER

How do you find a great Web designer? Check out existing sites to find those that appeal to you. Often the design firm is listed on the Website, or this information is available by calling or e-mailing the company.

What to look for in a designer? Evaluate the questions he asks about you. Are the questions creative or obvious? You need both. Has he done sites you respect? Tell him your brand and ask what he envisions your identity to be. If you're not happy with the answers, even after some discussion, you may not be on the same wavelength. Explore other collaborations. Quiz the designer for specific suggestions on the images and the words he would use for your site, but especially the visuals. Web media are not writer-friendly. The essential literary building block of the Web is the flash card. You've got to hit on content fast and move on to the next card, or beneath it to real depth, but getting to the depth for the viewer has to be a conscious choice, where he clicks on an icon and then sees text at essay length. Sites need to be archaeological layers of personality.

Buy the time of the best designer you can find for the front page. For subsequent pages, you can hire a college student or someone with less experience.

IN ALL THE OLD FAMILIAR PLACES

Of course, the soloist needs a few traditional identity instruments, like the letterhead. But even these take on new and lesser value in light of the Website and communicate not consistency but change and even temporariness:

- Letterhead. Designer Bill Drenttel is doing more with less: from his new country home, he uses his old NYC stationery with a black slash inked through the old address. Sometimes he writes a letter in e-mail format, prints it, and faxes it. That is a clear signal to clients that his identity is found online and not in a single, static piece of paper.

  Drenttel avoids the beautiful and overdesigned. He favours letterhead to which he doesn't give any thought. He wants clients to know that these things don't really matter to him, that his interests are broader and deeper.

- Business cards. Minimally functional cards are best. No one saves them; information is entered into a Pilot or other database organiser. The card gets tossed. Recognise cards' transitory nature and simply print up barebones cards with name, no title (you're you after all), location, and URL. Since I play with photography, I always keep a few duplicate shots on hand. When someone asks for my card, I pull out a 3 x 5 image of Soweto or a field and scribble my contact information on the opposite side. If the photo is interesting, chances are it—and my numbers—will be saved intact.

- Logo. "Look at how logos are used by corporations," says Bill Drenttel, who has redesigned *Newsweek* and now as a soloist is redesigning the Netscape browser. "They are overused by corporations and as a result, they've come to seem fake." Drenttel thinks the only logo a soloist needs is his own name, designed in a great typeface on good paper. "No more, no less."

If you must have a logo, have a few versions and vary their use. The publishing company Knopf has used a borzoi, a Russian dog, as its logo since its founding over fifty years ago. Some ten years ago, the borzoi changed with the kind of book published. On dramatic fiction, the dog would look sombre. On a comic novel, the dog would leap. On experimental non-fiction, the dog would be drawn as a stick figure. It was wonderfully playful, and early for its time.

Razorfish uses a mysterious logo that seems to change because it always looks different though it is the same. It's a small circle with edges pointing toward the inside. Thomas Mueller said it's the image of a gear, in stop-motion. When asked, "How many people at the company know that the logo is a gear?" he replied: "Not many. They mostly come up with their own explanations for it, which is good." Good, because it means the logo is simple enough to be memorable and mysterious enough for the viewer to make it his own with his own explanation. At different times the logo looks different.

This fits one of Marshall McLuhan's laws of identity. He said back in the 1960s that he was more attracted to a girl in sunglasses than to one in clear glasses. The girl in shades posed the greater mystery; he could complete her story himself. The same with a logo, should you choose to use one.

- Manners. Drenttel says, "The soul of a company is more about how you answer the phone than it is about your letterhead." Identity is in being known for prompt thank-you notes, or for acts of substance, like sending out a book that you mentioned in a conversation. Identity is in action, which again brings a solo to the Web.

But all this is window dressing on the Web. That's where the action is, that's where your counterpart, your professional soul, takes root and residency. The Web is your Walden Pond.

WEB FACES, WEB PLACES

As people are invited in to network and comment, your site will keep changing. Keep adding new copy, daily if possible. Otherwise, weekly or at least monthly. Experimenting with your identity and changing the site's contents, even its positioning, will attract visitors to your site and build loyalty. You can be bold in conservative ways, by being personal, as Avram is doing. Or by being professionally self-revealing, as I am doing, revealing the work of crafting of stories. Your mantra becomes "and" not "or." As a solo, you don't any longer have to be one thing to all people.

"Identity," as Bill Drenttel said, "is about control. To play with your identity and change it, not defend it as one thing, is the most powerful and open form of control. It's how you make the most of the opportunities open to you now."

Harness

16. Time Is Your Only Real Asset

You will make more money, attract more clients, become better at what you do as time goes on. The only factor you cannot increase is time itself. Well, you say, that's true for everybody. Maybe, but it's truest for solos. The problem is or will soon be that you *want* to do everything, not that you *have to* do everything. I want every opportunity that comes my way. Avram, in a state of near ecstasy as he set out to solo, said, "I want to pay attention to every opportunity that comes my way, because I feel it's come to me for a reason." He began investing in mediocre clothing boutiques because he met someone at a party. If a dog peed on his leg, I was afraid he'd move into veterinary medicine.

The temptation is to grab every opportunity (1) because you can, you're free! (2) because someone is beckoning YOU not your organisation—a total high, and (3) because for the first time work tastes like a cherry soda, and that is so groovy. Then you end up working sixteen-hour days and the hours don't feel like work, they feel like love. Until the endorphins wear off. Then they feel like insanity. Monstrous insanity. Westwood One radio host Jim Bohannon asked me, "Doesn't every soloist have the world's worst boss, namely himself, and no one to appeal to for relief?" If you've pushed people hard all your life, how do you stop pushing yourself?

Let me confess that I don't have the answer. I do have a bunch of solutions for the time problem solos face. They are not time management solutions. They are not workaholism repairs, since when you love something, your problem is the absolute opposite of workaholism. You don't burn out. You burn up! Solos are overworked *and* blissed out.

When I left Doubleday, I said to myself, "How great, I can break away for a latte anytime." I think I actually did that once, a year ago. One solo told me he was glad to be working against constant deadlines. "Otherwise I might stop for a drink of water." There was not a glint of irony in his voice. Even Hannibal Lecter was allowed water.

The best overall principle I have found for expanding time is this:

There was a silence for a moment . . . [Ernest] finally said, "Don't do what you sincerely don't want to do. Never confuse movement with action." In those five words he gave me a whole philosophy. I suppose the most remarkable thing about Ernest is that he has found time to do the things most men only dream about.

The speaker is Marlene Dietrich describing a phone call to her lover and mentor Ernest Hemingway. She is asking his advice on whether she should take a lucrative offer to sing in a nightclub in Miami. "Don't do what you sincerely don't want to do." That is the greatest time management principle. Writer/soloist Hemingway made a gift of it to singer/soloist Dietrich. How else did this Nobel and Pulitzer prize winning author have time to write in New York, Paris, Spain, to run with the bulls in Pamplona, to fish off the waters of Cuba, to marry three times, and to write mostly brilliantly, sometimes badly—except to live by that principle? When you are doing what you want, time becomes elastic. You can sit at a typewriter for ten hours and it feels like two, and in that time, you can perform with ease. You can converse with a client at noon, accomplish a reinvention of the world, and be shocked when your stomach rumbles to tell you it's dinnertime. You have nearly stopped time, and that's what has allowed you to fit in nearly everything. Because you don't think about what you've cut out. It never meant very much to you anyway.

Do what you want to do, and no more. That is what Hemingway means by action as opposed to movement.

A corollary to Hemingway's law is a practice of Dan Mapes's. Dan is a soloist who produced rock concerts for many years and is now leading an effort to build a theme park that is as virtual as it is physical—Oz in Kansas City, Kansas: "*Do what you love with the people you love,*" is Mapes's corollary. If you further narrow down your commitments to those conditions, you won't find yourself running short of time.

"When you are doing something that is a brand-new adventure, breaking new ground, whether it is something like a technological breakthrough or simply a way of living that is not what the community can help you with, there's always the danger of too much enthusiasm, of neglecting certain mechanical details," said Joseph Campbell about the hero's desire to press his solo experience for all it's worth. He was citing particularly the story of Icarus, solo flyer, who took off from the shore with this instruction: Fly the middle way, don't fly too high or the sun will melt the wax on your wings and you'll fall. Don't fly too low or the tides of the sea will catch you.

But Icarus, having left everybody else behind, and the earth as well, became ecstatic and flew too high. The wax melted and the boy fell into the sea. Just like a soloist to be claimed by his ecstasies and energy. The fall comes eventually. Campbell says the story means this: "When you follow the path of your desire and enthusiasm and emotion, keep your mind in control, and don't let it pull you compulsively into disaster."

Be aware that soloing will pull you into ecstasies. Choose only the work you really love. The work that, a year from now, you will be happy you chose to do.

Here are ways in which solos make those choices.

FIERCE ATTENTION TO A CORE PROJECT

With focus, you work hard, but without distraction.

The researcher and writer Ken Wilbur "gets up at three-thirty each morning to lift weights and meditate so as to stay in peak mental/spiritual condition to read through three or four heavy volumes a day," says his friend T. George Harris, founding editor of *Psychology Today*. Wilbur resists the distractions of fame such as book tours, media interviews, and foundation symposia organised to praise his works. He has rejected the ego protection of a nearly complete Ph.D.—in the biochemistry of cow-eye retinas—because Zen drove him to seek spiritual intelligence beyond the calculating mind. "An unrelenting workhorse," as George describes him, "Ken has plowed so many rocky fields of research and thought, Western and Eastern, that he is able to cultivate the long-lost hope of coherence. His drudgery provides a bold synthesis among researchers and scholars." This is focus of a laserlike kind. Wilbur goes deep.

Peter Drucker focuses too. He uses a preprinted postcard for turning down hundreds of invitations to make talks at big fees. He just checks off the reason that he can't do this one. A loner, Drucker refuses to build staff because managing is a waste of his time. He refuses to keep an office at the Claremont Graduate School, which set up the Drucker Management School. Why? Because if he kept an office at the school, he'd feel obligated to go to meetings, a colossal waste of time.

Drucker chooses projects that focus the mind so he can go deep rather than skim the surface where too many distractions are a continual threat. Summers he might spend reading only about China or Russian novels. The discipline gives him the feeling of inexhaustible time.

Consider how heroes pack their hours full. Winston Churchill in his solo life between gigs as prime minister used up every second. After the ladies came for lunch and the gentlemen came for dinner, Churchill stayed up through the night, often until four A.M., and wrote his books and speeches. His secretaries would say, "Mr. Churchill, it's getting dark," and he would reply, "That's usually what happens at night."

Churchill wrote eight volumes of *The History of Great Britain* and hundreds of magazine articles in those years when he was a soloist. When you pack your schedule with things you love/care about/want to pursue, you don't feel you are sacrificing anything but including everything.

Usually when a person chooses soloing, it's because he's seen the devil: A friend dies, a parent dies. You realise there's no time to waste. "Death is mankind's greatest gift," it's said, because when you finally realise that life is short, you become ferocious in using your time richly, not just productively. You stop spreading yourself thin. You think about the purpose of each commitment in your life. You put more items on a "reject" list than on a "to-do" list. Dan Mapes said that he doesn't even like to go to the movies any more because what he's doing in his real life is so much better. Choose what you love and it is possible to make your life more interesting than any movie.

MANAGING THE SELF

However hard I work as a soloist, however tough the project, it is a zillion times better than any meeting I remember at Doubleday. Those meetings, which had less and less to do with things I loved, went on at excruciating length. I was there by force, not by free will. What you do in freedom is never as onerous as what you do by command.

But all the hours a soloist puts into work can take a toll on the body, even if it leaves the spirit unscarred. You can wake up in knots, like fine macramé, but deny it because you're happy to go back to your work. Every day is a privilege.

Give yourself a bonus. A massage every week. Stress mounts in the body, and even exercise won't relieve it. Jonas Salk did sunrise yoga. Explore these avenues.

Book time for relaxation in your schedule, especially in your first six months. Just when you want to get a running start, book in more relaxation time than you think you need. Setting up a pattern from the beginning is important.

Mix your forms of relaxation. Doing this will help you become better at your work. Biographers say the great German philosopher Hegel could never have transformed philosophy without having walked five miles each morning. Martin Luther spent lots of time "in the tower"—the lavatory of the monastery. Such earthy meditations became so much a part of the constipated time of the monks that one of the little jokes on the capital of a pillar in the Toledo cathedral shows a monk who has been sitting on the "thunder mug" so long that a spider has spun a web from his bottom to the chamber pot. Mediation is supposed to stop time. If you're good at it, it does.

Delegate the bossing of you. I have two agents who make money from my activities: one is Sandy, my literary agent, who makes sure I'm not dangerously over- or underemployed. The other is my speech agent, who politely declines offers that are not of the first rank. Those two help in filtering assignments.

Other soloists call for help. It is not a sin, as a soloist, to hire extra help on a temporary basis.

MILLER TIME

Draw up a plan in which you decide how much time you will work and how much time you will devote to your life. "On my plan," Avram says, "a good day will mean no work. On a day when no one calls, I'll say, 'Oh, the plan must be working.'" He runs every opportunity through this screen of questions.

Here is how he chooses how to commit his work-time:

1. How do I feel about the people?

2. How do I feel about the ideas or mission?

3. What will be required of me?

- How much time?
- How difficult is it to reach the client's location?

4. What will I learn?

5. What conflicts will it create (with other professional work)?

6. What will I be paid?

These are the criteria by which Avram will accept an assignment into the 60 per cent of his schedule that is devoted to work. The other 40 per cent is devoted to health, music, public service, and friends and family.

"I haven't assigned strict values to these six items," Avram explains. "I would say that 1 and 2 have to be very high or I do not care about the rest; 6 sort of defines 3 through 5. If I get paid a lot of money, but not entirely, I can put in more time on an assignment, and have more conflicts about doing it, in which case it will not matter what I learn. This is all within reason.

"However, if I look at my actions, I would say that the money is not that much of a driver as long as it is good. I have the chance to make most money with one or two of my clients. But to the third I will give just as much effort because of my friendship with the CEO."

Avram had for a while considered partnering part-time with a Bay Area venture firm, thinking he would have more time if an established company handled his office work. Then he remembered the reason he wanted to go solo was to be able to make his own schedule and disappoint no one if he decides to take off a day and go to the beach. His time budget depends more on enjoyment of work—which he defines as learning and friendship—than of money.

But this schedule is also a marvel of strategy. By means of it, Avram has made himself a scarce commodity. He has made it clear to potential clients that he is devoting no more than 60 per cent of his time to business. By this declaration he has made himself a rare good. Having set severe limits on his time means that, perversely, everyone will want him; few will have him. His prices will reflect that.

PORTFOLIO TIME

The soloist can allow the calendar more elastic "give" by working on portfolio time, meaning variety: a mix of consulting, writing, board positions, philanthropic efforts, lecturing, goofing off. Time comes to seem like a enemy when you more or less do the same thing, week after week, season after season. Soloists break up fatigue (and boredom) by varying the kinds of work they do, each of which will draw on different time-muscles.

DON'T DISTRACT YOURSELF WITH FEAR

Historian Isaiah Berlin wrote of Franklin Delano Roosevelt that he had an "astonishing appetite for life . . . and complete freedom from fear of the future." A passionate faith in the future, confidence in one's ability to shape it, and a good eye for the truth—on these matters Roosevelt was a "genius," Berlin says. He calls this "the feeling of being at home in the present and in the future. It made up for FDR's faults of character or intellect."

I'd wager that corporadoes waste a lot of time daydreaming about sex. But solos waste as much time daydreaming about fear, lack of confidence, and other forms of negative thinking. These tendencies sap a lot of time and energy. I am always asking myself, "Do I need this fear; how does it serve me?" Fears demand letting go. Suddenly time expands.

Werner Erhard used to talk about how at the age of forty he gave up the Est empire he'd built and went solo: He became a race car driver. Alone in the cockpit of a car, he didn't have to manage anyone or be responsible for anything but himself.

He bought a car, got a teacher, studied, drove like a demon, and began entering races. After several months, he got so good he was placing third and fourth, then finally second. This thrilled him. But no matter what he did, he couldn't improve enough to win. He began to think it wasn't ability, it wasn't the quality of the car that made the difference between a first-place win and a second-place finish. So he decided to hang out with winning drivers to watch what they were doing.

He discovered that those who win are the ones who slow down time. They are, like FDR, "at home in the present." Werner found that the winning drivers sit in the driver's seat in the same relaxed state in which they sit at home in front of their TV holding the remote control. The car is going nearly 200 mph but in their minds and their bodies, these drivers are actually moving very slowly. That calm allows them to see the tiny grooves on the road's surface that should be impossible to see at such speeds, and aim the wheels into them. The grooves carry the car, thereby shaving one-tenth of a second off their speed—the infinitesimal amount that enables a driver to win.

Michael Murphy, founder of Esalen and author of a book about sports and time called *In the Zone*, says that "athletes in the heat of competition have a sense of amplitude." That sense of fullness and completeness calms them. That's how solos should feel: as if they've already won. As if the review for the film has come in and it's good. As if the meeting has already taken place, and they are allowed to feel triumphant. By working in that frame of mind—of already having won—you relax and make time slow down. Jackie Stewart, the famous race car driver, said that when he raced through the narrow, twisting streets of Rome on the Grand Prix, maneuvering his car at 180 mph, he was traveling so slowly mentally that when he turned a corner, he was able to see a rose growing out of the cracks in the wall. At 180 mph!

Michael Murphy explains this by saying. "When you alter time, you alter space. Einstein was talking about big objects—stars—when he invented his theory of time. But it relates subjectively to our experience as well. When you become contemplative, or learn to meditate, your sense of self alters. You become more self aware and aware of others in the world. You can see things. You have more reaction time. That's why time doesn't necessarily slow down, but your experience of it does. It's within the power of the human body to alter anything in the world." Murphy recommends siestas for solos. And rituals of leisure, like long meals. But most of all he recommends "just saying no" to opportunities.

Breathe deeper and time expands.

GOOFING OFF ON YOUR OWN TIME

Goofing off on your own time is tough to accomplish. But there are certain kinds of time off that are healing to the work-ravaged spirit.

Work that draws on a latent talent of yours is one

way to goof off on your own precious time. Push toward a dream that seems too big. It's so big you can't take it seriously, so you do it just for the sheer joy, the play of it.

For me it's writing a historical novel. Every success I have lures me away from that project, because the novel is so speculative. Assignments and projects and jobs crowd out my dream. But now I devote a few evenings a week to the novel, just for me. I have the experience of luxurious, unlimited, unencumbered time. In it, I behave like someone else. I treat this experience as a rehearsal: I carry that feeling over into my "real" work routine.

If distancing yourself imaginatively doesn't cut it, add in the physical dimension. Poet Carl Sandburg made his home in the mountains of North Carolina as part of a strategy to keep others from wasting his time.

Then too there is the beach, a latte, a movie in the middle of the day. Sometimes . . .

WHO/WHAT ARE YOU RACING AGAINST?

How do you know you're successful enough to throttle back on the pressure?

A standard-issue job tells you when you have succeeded: You're promoted and given raises. You measure yourself against a clear and public standard. But when you have no limits set on you, nothing to measure yourself against, you may never know when you've achieved success. You can work yourself sick.

In self-organised work, the only one you compete with is yourself. You're always butting up against your own limitations. A year ago, if I had a client, I would have spun myself into sugar. Now I have two clients, a board seat, just got invited to another board, and I'm wondering why I'm not on TV, why I don't have three new projects lined up, and asking constantly whether I'm working hard enough.

What's the point of soloing? One consultant told me, "It's to have no clients, just to be able to read poetry." "Not to work at all, but to travel," said a friend who is a poet and can read poetry all day long. The goal for a solo is to get so good at doing only what you love that work feels like play.

Because what does all this effort really amount to?

Hemingway thought he knew:

There are some things which cannot
be learned quickly, and time, which is all we have,
must be paid heavily for their acquiring.
They are the very simplest things,
and because it takes a man's life to know them,
the little new that each man gets from life
is very costly and the only heritage he has to leave.

We have one life. As Hemingway says, concentrate on "the very simplest things," because it takes a lifetime to know just these small matters, like the rose growing out of the concrete wall. To discover such epiphanies, remember, is in large measure why you went solo in the first place.

17. Love Like You've Never Been Hurt, Dance Like Nobody's Watching, and Work Like You Don't Need the Money

Soloists I know have earned twice their old salary, sometimes as early as their second year.

Solo money is a force unto itself. If you're doing things right, you could earn more on your own than you earned from any corporation. But you have to be completely reprogrammed. You're not in Salary Land anymore.

Salary money showed up every week and required minimal care and concern. Like some sacred relic, it is never touched. It disappears into direct deposit and exits just as mysteriously. Solo money is different: It is NOT cold hard cash. Every pound that leaves your pocket will have a name and a personality. You will wave it goodbye. Solo money will not show up by any time frame that can be considered "regular." When it arrives, sometimes after you've prayed for it, you will not fight the urge to kiss it, like some Scrooge who lives only for cash. You'll love it and fear it as you never had before.

But first it will make you obsessive. Avram, who never talked of money when he was at Intel, talked of nothing else when he just left paycheck land. I obsessed. For a year I was scared of going destitute. I had lived for those two Doubleday paychecks a month. But the solo checks were coming once every six months when they were coming at all. I started having hallucinations. Or were they hallucinations? A homeless man moved in across the street, on the street. Every morning I got up to write, he got up to write. Was he me? Was he a glimpse into my future? "What if I lose my house?" I cried to Bubba, who manufactures boxes for Compaq and offered to send me one in my size. "It's wax-lined," he said. "That should keep the rain off you."

George Bernard Shaw, the great playwright, had a stark lesson in how different salary money is from solo money. Young Shaw started a career in business and felt the threat not of failure but of success:

I made good in spite of myself, and found, to my dismay, that Business, instead of expelling me as the

worthless impostor I was, was fastening upon me with
no intention of letting go.

He was twenty years old with a steady future ahead
of him when "In March, 1876, I broke loose." He didn't
just go solo, says scholar Lewis Hyde, he went solo with
a vengeance: Shaw left family, friends, business, even
Ireland, his native home. He eventually succeeded on
his own. But first he spent eight years learning to
write—for no money, no steady anything.

Psychologist Erik Erikson said soloists like Shaw
have to go through some period of uncertainty—a
"moratorium"—during which they sometimes starve
themselves, socially and nutritionally, "in order to let
the grosser weeds die out, and make way for the
growth of their inner garden."

Solo money is the chance to change your thinking about
money. You have to, in order to do a little gardening of the
self and psyche. It's the chance to discover your worth, not
just your price, or what your company considers the price
of owning you. Price/salary: These are the measures we've
grown up with, the value by which we judge success.
These measures don't apply to the solo life or to the solo's
chance to earn his fortune. A painting has worth; the paint
that goes into it has a price. A solo is in a different league
making art of his work, not just a business. This is important in how you build your work, and bill for it.

In my experience and that of the solos I've met there are seven indelible laws of solo money. They govern you the moment you begin to think about your independence.

The Seven Laws of Solo Money

1. Measure Everything by How Much Life You Have to Give for It

This law is important before you make a move out of your company: Think about what you commit yourself to not just in financial terms, but by how much of your freedom you have to give up to afford it. Thoreau quit a nasty civil service job and went off to live on remote and pristine Walden Pond, to teach himself that the art of writing and the art of living were inseparable. He realised he had been a slave to many possessions for which he really had no personal need.

The cost of a thing for Thoreau was measured by how much life he had to give for it. "Measure life in loan payments and time quickly runs out," he said. If it took two months a year in a job he hated to pay his mortgage, he wouldn't buy but rent, or better yet, occupy. His aim was to "build more magnificently, and spend more lavishly than the richest, without ever impoverishing" himself. That meant cutting out things important only to the ego, and to go whole hog on things important to the spirit.

Love Like You've Never Been Hurt

List your big expenses and ask yourself if you had to cut any of them, would you be a different person and how would you feel about your life? Is your self-worth tied up in any of them?

2. The Price of a Ticket on the Freedom Train Is Nothing. It's Free

You're on the verge of leaving, or you've started on your solo career and are making a big financial commitment to its development. The law at work at this point is self-investing. It hinges on the relationship between money and freedom. While you were used to imagining costs in terms of a price, in the freedom space of soloing, "cost" is not a dollar amount. Cost is skin.

"How much does it cost to buy my freedom from an oppressive job?"

The man at the corner table of New York's Chelsea Bistro was telling his buddies, "The only money I care about is freedom money." He was saving like mad, he said, but the tone in his voice suggested he didn't think he'd ever accumulate enough money to quit his job. Just what is the magic number? What is "enough" money to cut the tie, to give a person the security to walk boldly into uncertainty?

If a ticket to freedom came with a price, that would be an easily negotiated passage, no matter how steep. Droves of people would pay it and be on their way out from under a dumb boss or an unfair system. Freedom, true to its name, is free. In terms of money. But it will cost you.

Free is not a number. It's a leap into the unknown. The French philosopher Jean Paul Sartre called freedom "nausea," and it is. It's scary. It feels like a freefall. You leap in a state of uncertainty. I couldn't compute what I'd earn as a soloist, because I'd never been a soloist. How would I know if I could afford my freedom? I didn't. I had to expect uncertainty.

Let's look at this in purely money terms. For that, you draw up two estimates: cash outlay and sources of revenue.

First, itemise your expenses for the first eighteen months, not twelve, of independence. Do this in order to give yourself a slightly longer runway to break even. In one column list the amounts of your basic necessities: mortgage, food, medical insurance, and enough mad money to maintain some elements of your former lifestyle so that in your first months of soloing you don't feel like a loser. In the next column, list the costs of startup soloing: Web design, business travel, health/life/disability insurance (as much as $5,000), office equipment, and office space if you can't work from home. Add up the totals of the two columns.

There will be expenses you have as a soloist that you never had as a corporate player: for example, in the US a self-employed person has to pay Social Security taxes. Normally an employer pays half of this amount and deducts the second half from your salary. When you are self-employed, you have to pay the tax on your own: 12.4 per cent up to $72,600 net gains, 2.9 per cent Medicare tax on all profits—in all, and an additional 15.3 per cent in "self-employment tax". A similar system operates in the UK.

I estimated basic cash outlay for eighteen months at roughly $100,000. I overestimated deliberately. Just to keep from drawing on my savings, I saw I'd need to earn $100,000 over the first eighteen months of soloing.

Next I estimated my sources of revenue, divided into two columns: a conservative estimate and an optimist's forecast for roughly eighteen months.

The third column indicated here was not part of my original forecast. I include it to show what I earned. My income for the first eighteen months hit a mid to high course between my conservative and optimistic forecasts. How did I manage that? I have to conclude that prophecy is reality. When I look at my real earnings, I wonder would have happened if I'd estimated even higher on the optimist's side?

To explain these earnings, keep in mind that I left the corporate world after twenty years, ten as a publisher and imprint founder. But as I've said, my reputation didn't matter much as a solo, because I was moving into

	Conservative	Optimistic	(Actual)
Book Earnings			
My first book—			
Princessa	$50,000	$100,000	($100,000)
New book	$75,000	$100,000	($150,000)
Retainer	$50,000	$50,000	($50,000)
Articles	$10,000	$20,000	($50,000)
Speeches	$25,000	$100,000	($25,000)
Consulting	$10,000	$30,000	$2,000
Totals	$220,000	$400,000	$377,000

different fields—writing and consulting—and I was entirely dependent on my earnings. I had no other source of income, like family or investments. All that lay between me and the streets was my ability to work. Also divide my totals by half, as half goes to taxes.

When I gave up my salary, both my conservative and optimistic sources of revenue looked too optimistic. For the short term, my income was pathetic: one lecture booked at $10,000 and the $50,000 Doubleday retainer. If I earned nothing else, I'd be drawing down on my savings.

Peter Drucker's rule of thumb is that it takes three years for any new business to climb into the black. By

Drucker's rule, a ticket on the freedom train would have cost me roughly $200,000: expenses/cash outlay for three years. That's no ticket to freedom; that's indentured servitude. That's why the price of a ticket on the freedom train costs more skin than money. Knowing the numbers only helps up to a point.

Calculating your income makes your earnings as real as your expenses. Knowing your expenses helps you contain, not exceed, them. Knowing your earnings sets a goal you can approach.

From there the cost is emotional.

3. Spending Is Having

Having is not accumulating. Having is spending.

The soloist's first impulse on winning her freedom is to be conservative in her cash outlay. Resist this terrible temptation to hoard. You're free. Let your spirit and faith in yourself expand. Watch your dollars and you'll be smaller and shabbier than when you left your job. As the poet Rilke put it, "Continuously squander all perishable values," of which money is one.

The success stories of the solo economy are all about using money as a jet uses fuel: burning it to get higher and higher. Spike Lee financed his first film on his credit cards. Darwin did his epoch-changing science with no salary and no institution to back-stop him. Francis Ford Coppola mortgaged his home and winery to finance

Apocalypse Now, one of the most legendary and profitable films of all time.

Coppola has always been a solo flyer, working outside the jurisdiction of the Hollywood film establishment. "If I spend $1,000 recklessly, it feels like $10,000. I never have pipe dreams," he says. If it's worth dreaming, it's worth doing.

Money is not security; your faith in your work is your security.

Spending is having; it's the artist's way, and soloing is more like art than like business: In Marrakech, the last city before the Sahara desert begins, the Ganawa musicians send audiences into a trance with their hauntingly beautiful sounds. They put out plates for contributions, *but money is not the point of their performance*. They are Sufis who worship God by playing for money. At the end of the ceremony, they take their earnings and spend every last cent that same day they earned it in order to begin the next day empty. To accumulate riches is a no-no. That would make them worry about their savings and their bills and would thus distract them from their music and from God. Earning the money is important: It connects them to their audiences and the real world. But letting the money slip through their fingers is equally important. Their music, not the money, provides the meaning of their lives.

By doing this they can concentrate on their music.

They can be selfless and give themselves the chance to go all the way. It is a radical method of cleaning out—of spending to have—that is characteristic of soloists in cultures closer to home. In less radical ways, soloists do the same.

One night seven years ago, the photographer Phil Borges went to bed as a successful orthodontist. When he woke up the next morning, he'd changed into a photographer, or rather someone who decided to quit his practice to start over again, solo.

Most soloists bring some of their skills with them from their past. But how does one go from orthodontist to photographer? The answer is: naked, giving everything away. "I sold my interest in the practice and got a payout over six years," Borges says. "I had a nest egg. Other than that, there was nothing I could plan. I couldn't say in four years I would be saving myself with this expensive hobby. I also started a family at that time. It was quite a bit of pressure, more than I needed."

A solo photographer, Borges doesn't do anything for the money. "The latest project I'm doing is a book for Interplast, an organisation formed by plastic surgeons thirty years ago. They do cleft palate surgery on kids who would otherwise never get this service. I wanted to help them. I looked at my time schedule and my budget, because I decided to do it pro bono. *All my projects are initially pro bono*. When I did the Tibetan project—a show and a book called *Enduring Spirit*—I did not get grants to go to India four times for the shoots. I used my own funds." That project was picked up by Amnesty International, which sponsored an international tour of the photographs, building an international reputation for Borges.

"I have the belief that when you do work that is close to your heart and you believe it is valuable in some way, it will come back in some way. So far that's been the case."

Burn your way to empty. I did: I blew my living expense money for nearly a year, taking almost no projects to work on spec on a book proposal. When it was rejected, I considered applying for a job filling donuts. Being struck with the stark reality of no prospect for income made me finally barrel through the proposal. It got sold. Once it sold, other assignments followed.

4. Risk Is the Way to Get Rich

You've done all the numbers. You've made the leap. How much more risk can you afford to take with the work itself?

It used to be that to succeed, a new business promised to deliver efficiency or quality. The most successful people today are promising the opposite: *not what's possible, but what's impossible*: Risk. Adventure. Internet companies like Amazon promise the new and unknown and work in negative cash flows to grow. People are getting wealthy not by building new services or products *but by producing occasions for risk.*

Every soloist is a risk taker, at the meta level, just by stepping out of the perfect pouch of organisations, and often at the work level, by choosing work that is also experimental, happenstance, or even, sometimes, slightly insane. A soloist's portfolio of work should include adventures, something that falls in the category of high risk occupations or projects. In the current economic culture, this small area may well turn into your biggest money-maker, perhaps because it is the source of your passion. (If it weren't, why would you even entertain the risk at all?)

How can you get paid for risks you are taking? Often for the story: not the adventure, but what you bring back.

Reinhold Messner is a solo climber, the Michael Jordan of his sport. "My mountain climbing has always been a way to put myself to the test. I've always gone where I met danger in an effort to test my skill." Messner has gotten rich, but he takes no money for climbing; to do that would, he feels, be to draw the anger of the gods who inhabit the mountaintops. Instead, Messner charges big fees to headline conferences where he tells the stories of how he faced Everest, solo, without oxygen, during the height of the monsoon, widely regarded as the greatest mountaineering feat of all time. There are surfers in Malibu who do what they love. People watch them just for the thrill, and sponsors pay their living costs, because audiences love to watch people in love with their work.

What's risky for you? The style of the investment fund you sell? Your project on city planning? Phil Borges has devoted a year to working on photographs of children who've had cleft palate surgery. These are not the glittery or edgy images found in fashionable galleries, but Borges is thinking only in terms of risk: how far out on a limb can he go, not how much money can he make. Ultimately you make more money by forging a risky path than by selling your services as a commodity. Sell ONLY commodity-safe consulting, customer service, for example, and you beg the question: Why should someone hire a soloist rather than a firm? But expand your practice to work too risky for most firms, and you have your trademark as a soloist.

5. In the Corporate Economy, Everything Has a Price—a Value. In the Solo Economy, Things—and You—Have Worth

There are two economies: a transaction economy, which is the world of plushy organisational Carpet Land. Everything there has a price. But the soloist lives in parallel world called "the gift economy." The gift economy doesn't run asccording to prices; it runs by a gift exchange: I give you my talents, you give me the fruit of yours. It's hard to put a price on one's worth. A painting, for example, has worth. It is not the sum total of $100 in paint and canvas. It can have a worth of many millions, because it doesn't just teach or supply. It touches people. This too is what a soloist does.

"In the presence of a person who recognises his own genius, others come to recognise themselves as the geniuses they are," writes philosopher James Carse. A soloist has recognized his uniqueness or his special worth; that's why he's taken a stand outside the corporation. *This declaration of your real worth is your real worth.* This is a part of the package a soloist offers: a gift that touches other people and potentially touches or alters their lives. You are your expertise; but as a soloist, you are also a model of the life of freedom, which is what people hunger for.

I have seen Avram move in this world. He is valued anew by customers and clients because he represents for them a life of independence which they want to have.

Before you think about your price, think about your worth. Think about yourself—or your gifts—as a gift.

We're accustomed to thinking that everything has a price. So the soloists' first impulse is to devise his fee structure. You can investigate what your peers get and charge accordingly. But this has terrible limits. For one thing, you are building a portfolio of activities, so you need different ways of billing. I write and consult and lecture and coach leaders and study strategy and poetry —sometimes all at once for clients. There is no way a soloist can bill conventionally for her range of work.

Clients would rather pay by time, because it's easier than negotiating. And because it's the familiar way. We live after all in a commodity or transaction economy. Go into Bally and buy a pair of shoes. You know you will never see the salesperson again. Nor do you want to. If she starts talking you up in a chatty way, you never go back. You just want the shoes. Everything has a price and you pay it. Similarly, a psychoanalyst charges to heal you. A set fee—determined in advance—is important so you don't confuse the relationship with intimacy, which would be detrimental to your therapy. That's the commodity economy. It's a world of alienation and disconnection, but also a world of low risk and low intensity. You can walk out of Bally leaving behind no skin. You come and go easily.

In a wonderful book on the subject of the gift economy called *The Gift*, author Lewis Hyde points out that there are times when people want to be treated as strangers. But clients drawn to soloists want occasions of professional friendship and closeness. One of my clients knows everything about my life, and I know about hers. We talk business and discuss strategy, but we also share stories of health and illness such as would once be shared only with friends. We are not equals but peers. We are not firm and client; we are involved in a different exchange.

To establish your worth, think of yourself as a gift.

6. Get Paid for Your Worth

Don't charge a fee, ask for a donation.

Preset fees can be impossible to determine. How can you know in advance what a task will be worth? You can't. It's the nature of gifts that the gifts become more valuable as time goes on. A preset schedule of fees limits the soloist's gift.

I recently helped X rescue an important project by giving him a new direction to take and putting him in touch with two experts I know, one of whom he's hired to execute the project. Doing this took a few hours of my time. Not much. But something. Those hours were worth more to X than to me. Do I ask for a consulting fee for that small amount of time?

Yes. Soloists are often called on to consult on their expertise, and because the callers think it's just a conversation, the subject of payment never comes up. It would be terrible to give the caller a bill. But compensation should be made on the order of worth.

The value of the service I provided X can't be measured by time as a conventional consultant, lawyer, or accountant would measure his value. I could ask for a percentage of what the overall project is worth—$5,000 to $10,000—as X pays one of my recommendees between $50,000 and $100,000 to complete his project. I could have stated my fees for service up front, explaining that the only asset a soloist has is her time, so I must charge.

But there's a prior question: Should I ask for anything? Should I simply wait for X to ask *me* if there is a fee for my time? He is used to paying for advice, why not my advice? If I make it clear that my time is worth something, I will value it more myself.

I finally said this to X: "I am starting a foundation. It is dedicated to founding a girls' leadership camp in Soweto, South Africa. In addition, it will fund a study of leaders engaged in adventurous assignments. I won't charge you anything for the work I'm doing for you. But if you feel it's helped you out of an impasse, I would appreciate it if you would make a contribution to my foundation."

A foundation? For a soloist? Yes. A person goes solo to educate himself, to deepen his mind and character and skills. Doing that by helping others is how exchange (not transaction) works. It is using your gifts to provide gifts to others. That is what a foundation does.

Gifts made to the foundation can be targeted to support research into topics the soloist champions. Starting a foundation dedicated to important new methods of understanding leadership will allow me to sponsor research and experiments. I can give the gift of the findings back to the world in the form of children's leadership camps in a country I care about. I can fund academic research on this topic. Findings and studies of both will come to me and make me a more important player in my field.

This is an example of a little person thinking big and playing big. The foundation and my request to X makes me more interesting to him. He doesn't just pay me off and go on his way as if he'd bought shoes at Bally. Suddenly his interests and mine converge in the mission of my foundation.

The foundation to start is one that is tax exempt, because people will give more when their donations are tax-exempt. But these are complex to set up. The Inland Revenue loses money on tax-exempt foundations, so it guards very carefully who does and doesn't qualify. It takes roughly twenty hours or two full days to pull together the necessary application forms and do follow-up work. A lawyer needs to help with the process.

But you don't have to start from scratch. In the last few years, people have begun setting up "earmarked funds" at large, established foundations. Community foundations like the Jewish Federation, or the American

Bar Association—if you're a lawyer—make these services available. Investment banks like Salomon or Lehman Brothers are also offering this as a service to their wealthy clients. You can ask your customers for pledges and when you have accumulated perhaps $100,000 in pledges, you can go to the foundation of your choice and say, "I want to set up an earmarked fund"—a custom foundation where you make the investment decisions. If your foundation grows, you may even hire your own staff.

Most people you help will contribute, because they know that if they need you again, they will want to keep the doors open. In the competitive corporate world, altruism—the highest form of giving—is a highly repressed emotion. But in the solo economy, altruism is unblocked.

A study in the United Kingdom found that people respond more generously when they think in terms of giving gifts. Americans are paid for giving blood, but in Britain, people donated blood, and per capita, the blood supply in the United Kingdom exceeded the supply in the United States. Then the British Red Cross changed to a pay-per-pint system and donations fell off dramatically. When a soloist requests payment as a gift, he changes the engagement from transaction, cool and complete, to an ongoing more intimate relationship.

Give your product away for free. But sell your service.

How can you survive if you give your work away? Very handsomely. And in the process you compete against the big boys.

A group of advisers explored the possibility of setting up a for-profit institute to teach new ideas in leadership. The problem was how to get potential client companies to pay $25,000 a year to join the institute. The venture capitalist in the group did a sophisticated mathematical projection. The ad exec thought about raising money through mail shots. Suddenly the VP of human resources at Microsoft asked, "What if we didn't charge charter participants for the first year? What if we invited them in for free?"

No one spoke. Her question stunned the group into thinking in a completely different way about the institute and about themselves: Suddenly the group was not selling anything. *There was the spirit not of work, but of play. They were giving, out of their largesse, out of their fullness.* That is the way writers feel when they deliver themselves of a novel, or painters when they release a painting from their mind's eye onto canvas. The Microsoft executive's comment led the group to junk the tired old formulas of education and draft a bold new charter.

What can you give for free—part of your service, or a free day of advice? It might be a study outlining your solution to a client's problem. Whatever it is, it will put you in a different frame of mind. "Free" will help you think out of the box. I know a consultant who is always giving away his ideas for new businesses. "I give away my ideas all the time. I don't know how to sell my ideas or how to charge for them. I say to people, 'If you do anything with that, I'd like a little stock in your company.' Or I'll mention an idea and the person will say, 'That's great. Can you help me develop this idea?' Then I'd sell my services."

What to charge for is as important as what amount to charge: Linus Torvalds, the creator of Linux, the most popular free software, offers a new operating code, and offers it for free—a direct threat to Microsoft. Linux is not only free, many consider it better than Windows because it is an open system that users can debug and then share.

Linux is the soloist's mission to crush Microsoft. How did Torvalds, a soloist, achieve such success going up against an established power? By putting his efforts only into "the kernel"—into Linux's most vital code. "It's one per cent of the entire program. Of that one per cent, I've written between 5 and 10 per cent. I think the most important part is that I got it started. Then people had something to concentrate on." At least 2,000 people have worked on the code for no salary. They've made Torvalds's project their own. They've invested themselves in it. "I didn't ask for this army of

Love Like You've Never Been Hurt

people to come to me," Torvalds says. "They come because this is what they want to do." Torvalds's profits come from selling the service to maintain the software, at $50 a package.

What is the kernel in your soloing proposition? Maybe it's an idea, or a technique, or a style. Whatever that is, give it away everywhere and anywhere. Write about it. Invite others to use it, share in it, develop it in their own style. Success in the new economy occurs when a lot of people copy your work. By then you are known as the source. Your service will carry the premium.

Achieve your worth steadily.

Give your product away, but what do you charge for the service? As mentioned, Allan Kennedy, a former McKinsey consultant, says a top-of-the-line consultant charges between $5,000 and $10,000 a day plus expenses or $500 per hour. If that sounds like a lot, ask for equity. New businesses are often worth a lot, especially if they go public or are sold.

Ask for equity. Avram made this offer to a small cash-starved startup he has been advising. He told the young CEO, "I want the option to buy $25,000 worth of stock at today's price and ninety days in which to do so. I also want to be on your advisory board, with a grant of additional stock." In this way, a soloist creates an upside.

7. *Cash Flow Is Life Itself*

You need money coming in to eat and make your dreams real. How do you ensure this? Retainers from the company that you negotiate on departure is one source of revenue to pay the bills while you hunt up new business. Retainers can range from a one-month to a one-year agreement the company offers you to continue to work with a few clients and be available to them.

For the times you need cash, charge as much as possible. I find the best way to say to someone that you must charge him is to explain that the only asset a soloist has is her time, and you need to turn the interaction to the benefit of your career. I often give clients a choice: barter or cash. I asked one potential client who is active in television ventures to consult with me on how to get onto television or consider paying my fee. He said he would be happy to do both.

I have learned that it's important to ask for everything. Ask for little and people feel devalued. Ask for a great deal and they feel honored to be thought capable of such largesse.

If the help you are asked to provide seems endless, offer to turn the day rate into a retainer: your daily rate for every day and a half, say, provided the client commits to booking you at three days a month. That guarantees you steady income, and the client gets a reduction on your fee. The client pays this amount whether or not he uses those three to five days.

The last gasp is that of independent filmmaker Robert Rodriguez, who made his breakthrough film, a Mexican spaghetti called *El Mariachi*, at age twenty-three at the cost of only $7,000. To earn the cash, Rodriguez became a human lab rat in a drug experiment. He bled twenty-four times a day, every hour, even when asleep, for a month. It was a windfall. "I didn't want money to stand in the way of doing [the film] right." And: "If I'm going to do [something], I really do have to go all the way or I'm wasting my time." The best thing about not having a crew, says Rodriguez, is that you have no budget. If you have no budget, you can't go over budget.

To stake yourself during times of low cash flow, there is a lot of freeware out there for solos:

Free advice. Barter your services. Solicit some clients based on your needs. A Web design company may need your help in marketing or accounting in exchange for a Web site design. If you have a business problem, your local graduate school of business may have a program by which students can get credit for work-study projects. Your problem may qualify. Send a proposal to the business school dean.

Free promotion. Write an article on a subject that you want to learn about and interview experts. You'll become known as an expert in the area where you knew little.

Free funds. Create a stock exchange called you. Entrepreneurs attract investors into their business because they have assets and a plan and projected profits. Start your own stock exchange. Sell shares in you and in your prospects. Invite initial investors—friends and others —to come in at a reduced price. Then increase the value of shares in you as your profitability goes up. A friend said he heard Eric Raymond speak recently and wanted to hire him for a day's tutorial on what Eric, one of the fathers of open systems software, knows. But Eric is something of a hippie and my friend didn't want to insult him by offering either too much or too little. If Eric had a stock exchange he would have bought shares and gotten his advice.

Free ride. Taxes will eat up your income if you are not careful. A soloist can have money coming in, and then four times a year see up to 60 per cent of it go to taxes. How do you avoid this? Claim as expenses nearly everything, including office space and furnishings and business meals and subscriptions. Remember too that before you accept a job you think you are doing just for the money, only half of your fee is yours. The rest goes to taxes and your accountant. (See also the chapter "How Not to Work for Your Uncle.")

The laws are the laws. Stray from them, and you invite financial trouble, later if not sooner. This is so because these laws of solo money maximise your confidence and take advantage of the changes happening in the new economy, which doesn't work like the old economy. You, soloist, are there at the raw edge of the frontier. The laws of solo money will help you keep justice on your side.

And so will hiring an accountant and lawyer who are willing to invest in you and who will see you as an important relationship. Hire a soloist accountant. Make your whole "staff" other soloists, so you can grow in the business together and barter and trade if and when money gets tight, especially in the first years when you are working too hard to build your practice, and the last thing you need is to keep your own books.

In solo land, money isn't just money. It's karma.

18. Security Measures

"What if something happens to me and I can't work? What do I fall back on?" I ask Avram. "That's what disability insurance is for," he says. Of course! Health coverage is automatic when you leave Ma-Pa corporation, but disability insurance is the invisible umbrella. You have to find and buy these protections yourself. I check the Web for insurance brokers but decide to find someone I can trust. I call my accountant for a recommendation and soon reach his broker, who asks for my last three years of income tax returns, my book contract, and notes on other sources of income before coming back with an estimate: Maximum coverage means $8,000 per month, starting forty-five days after the onset of disability, until death. The premiums, he warns, are enormous. Coverage will cost roughly $9,000 the first year, and escalates by a thousand nearly every year after that. I have no idea if this broker's estimate is high so I must try for a competitive bid.

Of course Charles Manson shows up in my daydreams.

When I first left the company, I hadn't thought about disability insurance. Suddenly it became all I think about. I decided to get two more bids. But both come back with a higher premium, and more dire warnings: "Buy insurance now while you're still under the Doubleday retainer contract, otherwise you may not seem a good risk." Meaning: An employee is safer than a soloist. As a woman I am already disadvantaged in the eyes of the insurers. Women live longer than men but have more medical complaints.

I finally decided to apply for a policy that kicks in after ninety days, which is less expensive. The monthly indemnities range from $7,000 to $8,000. The frustrating part is that they do range, and it's difficult to know why. Even after the broker's lengthy and confusing explanations. How to choose?

Insurers make an important distinction in policies: There is non-occupational disability insurance, which pays out only part of the policy if it's determined that you're able to work in some other occupation for the time you are disabled. The better policy is occupational disability insurance. It pays out the whole benefit if you're disabled to the extent that you can't perform your occupation: if, say, a dancer breaks his leg.

If you think Harvard's tough, try getting occupational disability insurance. The procedure involves a medical exam, tax records, and a lengthy application process. Start the process well in advance of the time you need it, so there is no disruption in coverage. I heard a lot of stories like the one of the doctor who left his hospital's employment to start his own practice. The very next day, he was hit by a car. He wasn't yet covered by his new policy.

Disability insurers want you to think they are doing you a favour by extracting a high premium every year to cover your income in case you cannot work. On the face of it, these policies look alike. There is a benefit period, a monthly indemnity, a residual disability rider, and a cost of living allowance geared to inflation. But the trick is the way the insurers define your "occupation"—can you do all of your job or part of it if disaster strikes? I consider myself a writer: If I can write but not travel, my income drops since "writing" is contingent on travel and reporting. But some companies evaluate travel as inessential. If I lose my sight, I can still write, but the difficulty mounts, wages fall; would insurance kick in?

The best policies define your occupation entirely in terms of the money you have earned over the last three years. Every broker spins his own veil of jargon over you, and you have to thoroughly question the definitions. The broker who said I should get insured fast as a Doubleday employee didn't say that if I become disabled after my contract ended—it was up for renewal on July 31—the insurer can refuse to award me a claim because my potential change in status was known to me but undeclared. You hide anything from the insurers only at your own risk.

I finally did get coverage, but by Lloyd's, the firm that insures the uninsurable, like the Hope Diamond and the ship the *Titanic* (not the mega-hit movie). I could get only a three-year policy, which means I will have to face the whole renewal process again soon.

BUSINESS COVERAGE

Saved the best for last.

Make sure you are not relying on personal insurance to cover business exposures, especially if you are working from your home. If clients meet with you there, or if you hire a temp for word processing or filing, you could have a "premises liability" problem with members of the public and workers who come to the house if they fall or injure themselves in any way.

You might consider getting a general liability policy

that covers bodily injury and property damage. Home-owners' policies covers you for small office work, like protecting you against the person who gives you piano lessons and your child's baby-sitter. But once "the public" walks into your home, the coverage is not broad or deep enough.

Some insurance companies are starting to offer home office addendums to homeowners' insurance policies.

If you have anyone working for you in your home even sporadically, consider getting worker's compensation insurance. Soloists generally will not need this. But if you had a florist shop and wanted to sell rare herbs from your garden which meant having someone come by to water them, then you should consider this insurance.

Hiring a person from a temp agency circumvents a lot of these risks.

As a soloist, you have to play sentry for yourself. Insurance is the one area in which you must be secure, so you can take real risks in other important arenas.

19. How Not to Work for the Taxman

Douglas Adams, author of the fabulously successful trilogy, *The Hitchhiker's Guides to the Universe*, was a soloist for a long time. His first paying job was providing security for a Saudi royal family visiting London. That required him to spend all night sitting outside their hotel door, watching the elevators come and go. Does life get more solo than that? His second job was scripting the radio programs that later became *H2G2*, as he calls his best-selling trilogy. I asked him why he decided to start a small Internet company after many years of soloing. It was a lonely life, he said. But worst of all was the one eternal presence he never managed to banish: the tax man.

He warned me: "If you write one successful book, you'll have to write a second just to pay taxes on the first. And then you'll have to write a third to pay taxes on the second." As a soloist, I've found taxes to be as big a burden as Douglas predicted. A soloist has to pay them four times a year, not once as a corporate person does. And just when you think you're doing fine, half of everything you earn gets shipped off to the taxman, leaving you feeling you could have done just as well by working half-time.

But you don't have to feel so dire just because you think you're working solely for the taxman and not that Honda Civic you so want to buy. There are measures you can take to shelter your income.

ISAS

There are a number of financial plans on the market that can be used to shelter a soloist's income and which may in many cases provide handsome tax-free returns. Prominent among these are Individual Savings Accounts (Isas) — the 'tax-free wrapper' savings schemes that replaced the popular Personal Equity Plans (Peps) and Tax-Exempt Special Savings Accounts (Tessas) on April 6, 1999.

Any UK resident over eighteen can take out an Isa and any investments held within it are free from income tax or capital gains tax and do not need to be declared on a tax return. Up to £5,000 may be invested in any tax year – the exception being the first year (April 6, 1999 to April 5, 2000) when up to £7,000 may be put in. This may be invested in a lump sum or by regular contributions.

Contributions are invested in a spread of financial assets, though there are some restrictions. £1,000 may be invested in cash (£3,000 in the first year) including bank or building society deposits, National Savings or money funds run by some unit trust groups. A further £1,000 may be used to buy life assurance. The £3,000 balance, or the entire maximum subscription of £5,000 (£7,000 in the first year), may be invested in stocks and shares, including unit trusts, investment trusts and direct equities.

An important difference between Isas and Peps concerns the income benefit of holding UK equities. Before April 6, 1999, holders could reclaim under the Pep wrapper tax credits on dividends from UK equities equivalent to 20 per cent. But from April 6, 1999, this has been cut to 10 per cent and will be scrapped in 2004.

The money invested in an Isa may be managed by an investment house, bank, building society or insurance company, all of which offer Isas on the financial market. More than one company can look after your annual contributions.

One option is to choose a maxi-Isa run by a single

company. Up to the maximum £5,000 per year may be invested, though the operating company does not have all three investment options – cash, equities and insurance. All it has to offer is the equities option; it may choose whether to provide the others.

A second choice is a mini-Isa, which allows three companies to manage each separate investment component of your money – a building society to manage the cash element, a friendly society or insurance company to manage the insurance component, and an investment house to take care of equities. Mini and maxi Isas may not be mixed in a single tax year; however, you may take out a mini Isa in one tax year, followed by mini Isas the following year.

From April 6, 2000, holders have the right to transfer their plans to another provider if they are not satisfied with the way they are performing or being managed. These transfers will not affect permitted Isa contributions. And unlike Tessas, Isas allow withdrawals without altering a plan's tax-free status.

The government has said that these products will be available for at least 10 years. Solists will therefore be able to invest a maximum of £52,000 up to 2009 – £7,000 in the tax year ending April 5, 2000, and £5,000 per tax year thereafter. The Treasury has also said it will review Isas after seven years to see if any changes need to be made after 2009.

ACCOUNTANTS

Among the first things UK soloists should do is to put a meeting with an accountant and an independent financial adviser at the top of their 'must do' list.

An accountant will advise on the best way to go about letting the Inland Revenue know of your plans, and will explain the numerous advantages – and some of the disadvantages – of becoming a sole trader. They will point out the tax breaks available to soloists – such as claiming relief on the part of your home that you use as your office – and give detailed information about how your change in status will affect the National Insurance Contributions you will have to pay.

It may be that turning yourself into a limited company will offer you greater protection than merely operating as a sole trader and, of course, there is always the thorny question of whether you should register for VAT.

Is it better to lease-purchase a car on the business, or should you go ahead and buy one outright? And what about travel costs, mileage allowances and the like? How do capital allowances work? Can you write-down the cost of any office equipment you need, such as computer hardware and software programs? An accountant worthy of the profession will have ready and informative answers to these questions.

FINANCIAL ADVISERS

An independent financial adviser will be happy to show you a wide range of financial plans – some good, some bad – on the market today. These include personal pension plans, unit trusts, investment trusts, investment and 'with profit' bonds, open-ended investment company investments (Oeics), friendly society savings schemes, plus tried and trusted old favourites such as National Savings and bank and building society accounts.

The average soloist will find that these products, with their complex mix of premiums, benefits, tax breaks, charges (both upfront and hidden), represent a bewildering and frightening arena. Though it is a good idea to try to acquire a basic knowledge of these matters, soloists are best served by choosing a reputable adviser – the best ones often come by personal recommendation from friends and colleagues – and letting the professionals do their work, which is to find you the best possible deal for your requirements and circumstances, and to save your precious money.

One product that deserves closer attention is a personal pension plan, not least because it represents an extremely important financial aspect of soloing – the day when you can take down your brass nameplate and set off on that world cruise or trek through Nepal you always promised yourself! As soloists start out on the

How Not to Work for Your Uncle

journey to become masters and mistresses of their own destinies they leave behind them the protective financial custody of their companies or corporations. Often they are members of a company pension scheme, and leaving the next to go solo means giving up this comforting retirement cushion too.

Taking out a personal pension is one way of continuing to provide for retirement. You make contributions each month and tax relief is allowed at your highest rate. Plans are offered by banks, investment and insurance companies, direct telephone providers and may now be bought through supermarket and High Street store chains.

In 2001, the government will introduce its stakeholder pensions – cheap and simple retirement savings plans aimed at those who can afford to put away only small sums each month. But newly free soloists should not wait until then to take out a personal pension – they should act now so as not to miss out on valuable tax relief. Holders of such plans will be able to switch to a stakeholder pension when these become available.

In view of the wide range of pension plans on the market and the bewildering variety of charges, benefits and conditions levied by pension providers, soloists should always consult an independent financial adviser before committing themselves to any product. They will search the market on your behalf to find the best possible deal and will point out those companies which impose high upfront charges, have a poor investment record and which offer poor value for money.

Remember – you act in haste, but repent at leisure!

MOST IMPORTANTLY . . .

This is a complicated arena, and not one the startup soloist should be spending his time studying, except for knowing the basic rules of what is and isn't tax-deductible. Says Denis, a tax planner: "I recommend that anybody going on their own find an accountant or tax lawyer to structure their business in order to maximize the income tax deductions. Sole proprietors need to know whether they should form a limited company. A planner will advise you on what is the best entity to create given the business you're in.

"Anyone who tries to get their head around this and to learn it instead of paying attention to the work they love is doing themselves a disservice.

"If you're good at making money, you should not be dealing with how to shelter it."

Surprise and Delight

20. What I Learned Without Adult Supervision

In the course of writing this book, I've examined the solo life more closely than I would have had I only lived it and not reenacted it for others. Laying myself open for self scrutiny, I've noticed some surprises that would otherwise have been missed in the rush of events. These surprises in particular stand out:

1. When I began *Soloing*, I thought the most important lesson was how to build a sole-practitioner business. I realise now that the most important lesson is in how to take care of yourself—your mental and physical health. You have to be watchful that you don't overcommit

to others or undercommit to yourself. Do that, and the business takes care of itself.

2. Quantity of work is not important. Quality of assignments is. I was impressed at the beginning when a lot of work rolled in the door. Now I realise that the work grows the soloist. Every assignment is a chance to be smarter as well as to keep the wolf from the door. Choose opportunities wisely.

3. The most important client, a friend cockily told me, is no client. Then he panicked. "Don't quote me," he begged, fearing his clients would be hurt if they learned he didn't really want them in his life. He meant that having got rid of a boss, he'd love to get rid of his other masters. "I want the time to write poetry, to do nothing if I choose." Soloing makes you realise you can do more with less: With fewer clients you can have more impact, because the relationship goes deeper and extends to each other's lives and communities. No client may be best. But I'd amend this lesson:

4. Your best client is yourself. Supporting yourself by doing what you love to do seduces you into doing it more and more, and doing as little of anything else as possible. I tried for a long time to win a famous CEO as a client. It was like banging my head against the Berlin

Wall: It was painful AND there was no wall. Now I just care about pleasing myself.

5. People will continue to think of you in the role in which they know you best. People are always seeing me as an editor because that's how I'd built my reputation. This limits a soloist's effectiveness. I still remember the dinner at which I was asked to give a talk about my work. The host introduced me by saying I would speak about the great authors I'd published. Instead of correcting him, I abandoned my text about my new work and talked about my old life. The memory of that still smarts. It still takes an effort to convince people to see a soloist as something new.

6. Soloing is the hardest work I have ever done. But it's also the most satisfying. Therefore the hardest work can also be the least tiring, the least depleting.

7. I have given up on my mania for security. Soloing is security—the security of being content with myself. As a solo, no one is judging me, finally, but me.

8. The practice of soloing is more Zen than Zen. Soloing builds you up and breaks you down at the same time, like those legendary masters who throw students into the mud on their way to enlightenment. As a solo,

you become more fixed in your ways but more open to systems, to destiny and fate. You realise that your power is only strength, that will counts for nothing, but appreciation for everything.

9. Nothing but the best suffices and you bleed over everything that does not make the grade.

10. Once a soloist, always a soloist. You can go back into the corporation, but the corporation can never get back under your skin. You can be paid, but not paid for.

DOUBLE ONE

There is one more lesson, the odd eleventh. When you solo for a period of time, you risk becoming less and less a business person because the world opens up to you and suddenly fresh opportunities come to you. The art of soloing seduces you. What was a way to do business becomes a way, a path, to the rest of your life. The business part turns into the husk you leave behind. The world opens up, you open up, and bingo, the music you wanted to write starts to be written. The play that's nagged at you starts writing itself in perfect dialogue. The desire to go back to veterinary school has you filling out applications. Soloing is a seduction for which there is no relief but consummation.

I told my friend Michael Hopkins my dream, stupid

and crazy: to disappear for a year and write a novel. He said, That's fine if you can afford it.

Can I afford it? No. Can I afford not to do it? No. So will I afford it? Yes.

I don't know how. But I'm going to start and believe I will find my way to financial success. I do not have a Plan B. But if I should need one, I will trust myself to come up with something. After all, I've proven I don't need adult supervision.

Soloists make a long circuit, but guess what? Most of us end up circling back home. Home is one's earliest dreams, before they got corrupted by "can't," "shouldn't," or "maybe later." I mean that the dreams we start with are the dreams we come back to—dreams that are a year old, or thirty years old. Postponed dreams. Like leaving Intel to work on his own in San Francisco near the street where he grew up, Avram's dream. My brother's boyhood dream to collect and sell military memorabilia. Phil Borges's dream to make the least comforting images the most beautiful. Dreams at the end of dreams. Extravagant dreams, to use Thoreau's adjective: not the dream of the wandering buffalo on his migratory, hardwired wanderings, but the path of the cow that toppled over the fence because she heard the bleating of her calf. The dream that seems to take you out of your path but really puts you right where you want to be. Maybe Richard Nixon should have realised his aim to be a sportswriter, the way Martha Stewart realised her dream to be America's arbiter of taste.

That's what happens when you solo. The world sees a brave individualist. And you see yourself without illusion. Illusion gets stripped away when you solo, because you don't have a big organisation and lots of co-dependents called colleagues to help sustain it. You see for the first time what you really should do, and what you can legitimately do. It's a rude awakening. All these years I thought I could be a business mogul, a counsellor to leaders. Fill in the blanks to describe your own sense of yourself. Maybe I can be these things. But soloing has also taught me that I can do what I want and probably make a go of it. So why delay that homeward mission?

We end up going home. It's not so strange that we should, or that soloing should hurry us on the road that brings us back to where we began.

Nobel laureate in fiction Italo Calvino once said a person needs to know ten things to equip himself for the future. One of them is the ability to take to the heights. But in a certain way, Calvino said:

Be as light as a bird, not as a feather.

Life is a solo flight. Now and then, it may look like there's a lot of traffic on the big blue skyway. But really

it's just you. And the way leads home. That's where
Thoreau left off: back home.

That's where you wind up in the passage from being
"on your own" to being "complete in yourself."

Resources and More

Here are the keepers of the plums, the holders of the goodies: the advice solos need for further help and information on your journey.

Solo Guru

Peter Drucker's memoir, *Reflections of a Bystander*, tells how the great soloist shapes his identity.

Break-up Lawyer

Jonathan Sacks
New York City

Solo Teacher

Linda Amiel Burns
The Singing Experience
New York City

Models for the Higher Voice

Erik K. Erikson, Young Man Gandhi

Brand Doctor

Tom Peters, "You Are the Brand" essay in *Fast Company*

Fernando Flores, BDA, Emeryville, CA, www.bda.com

Identity Shaper

Razorfish, Thomas Mueller, creative director,
www.razorfish.com

Gerry Brown, San Diego, CA, www.tinstring.com

Money Manager

Denis O'Sullivan

Mason Companies, Reston, VA

Time Management Adviser

Esalen Institute, Mike Murphy's *In the Zone*

Sources of Inspiration

The Gift, by Lewis Hyde

Voyage of the Beagle, by Charles Darwin. A scientific
odysssey and a lovely vision of discovery.

Insight into the Solo Arts

Project work: *60 Minutes*

Relief from Temporary Loneliness

Staff up with Information Processors,
www.infoprocessors.com

Research

World Future Organisation

How to Fit the World into the Palm of Your Hand

Eve Johnson's website, www.evesgarden.com

Utopia Parkway: The Life and Work of Joseph Cornell, by Deborah Solomon. Insight into the life of a great miniaturist.

Best Balm Against Rejection

A course in creative writing, painting, photography

Appearance at an open casting call (read *Back Stage* magazine want ads)

Best Defense Against Aloneness

Fast Company Real Time conferences

Best Example of Life After Soloing

Nominate yourself. Contact: www.thesoloist.com

THE BEST OF THE BEST . . .

That is reserved for a board seat. You get to spout opinions and be spared having to act on them. You can help a company grow and prosper, or nurse it through tough times in a state of wise detachment. If you get aboard a company about to go public, you stand to make a lot of money.

How do you get on board a company? Avram suggested I ask everyone I meet to tell me if he knew of an open position or if he could refer me to someone who might. You'd get a lot of rejections that way, but if you persisted, sooner or later an opportunity would come your way.

Mine did in June 1998 when I got a call from Margaret Heffernan, CEO of The Password. I heard Margaret's name first from Dave Wetherell, who is the CEO of The Password's holding company, CMGI. I'd asked him the question, and he said yes, one of his boards needed another member.

Margaret is creating magazines, zines, on the Web. She is no small thinker. She craves radical solutions. She believes the Web can become its own medium, not just another means of content delivery. When I met her, I was dazzled. "Maybe this will work for both of us," I thought. She promised to think about how we can work together. That was the first round. We agreed to meet again soon.

Margaret defined the board member's role this way: "CEOs are lonely. They can't tell their people of their outrageous ideas or ideas for the future without scaring them, without them saying, 'We've just jumped through this hoop, now you're thinking of something else?' I need someone smart to bounce ideas off. I need contacts, if I want to investigate some new approach. I need someone to tell me, candidly, if an idea is good or if it stinks."

A board seat is a good way for a soloist to make money. You stand to profit especially when the company goes public. In The Password's case no salaries are paid to board members. Margaret is offering me 25,000 shares. What is a share worth now? What could it be worth if the company is sold?

There are three kinds of boards. This one, The Password, is a private company that if sold will mean money in the bank. The reason to take this offer is my great respect for Margaret. I want to help her and the company, and I want to get experience in how to serve a board.

There are two other kinds of board seats. The second is the blue-chip board, which may pay in rubles but is still great because of the prestige, the reach of the company, and the contacts. Just being associated with such a board is hot. Avram, for example, had a seat on the KingWorld board until the company was sold to CBS. The third is the public affairs board, which keeps reminding you that business is a small subset in the larger world. This is crucial. If everything you do is for dough or rep, you stop learning. I would love to serve on a public affairs board.

Just to check, I called a friend to find out if the offer of 25,000 shares, no salary, was fair. He says it may be fair, but it wasn't great. He suggested I negotiate by asking Margaret some basic questions, good questions for any potential board member. They are:

- How many shares are outstanding on a fully diluted basis? (If there are 250,000 shares, my shares are valuable, but if there are 25 million shares, my shares are worth nothing.)

- What is the strike price of the options?

- Over what period of time do the options mature? (If it takes ten years, this is not an attractive deal for me, because I need cash now, and would get it if the company goes public or is sold. The content game is moving too fast, and the small players who don't have their own personality will be bought up, as Salon was bought up by Microsoft.)

- Is there early maturity, in case of change of control of the company? (If another company buys Password, more than likely membership of the board will change, and I do not want to lose my shares.)

- Am I able to keep the options if I am no longer serving on the board?

I also check with a member of the Internet content community, who gave me an unbiased review of the company and its product. He says it's trying to be all things to all people, that it seems to have no focus, that

335

it is a K-Mart kind of site, with lots of bargains but nothing edgy or cool to draw a person in. He confirms my instinct that the product needs celebrities and excitement to stir up interest. The exchange here will be my insight into content for experience in the online world. It sounded like a good trade as long as I am not disadvantaged in the financial deal.

A little more due diligence reveals that a board member should receive one per cent or a half of one per cent of the company in stock as compensation. From Margaret's reply, I am receiving a quarter of a per cent, which is low. If you get a low offer, ask the offering party why. If they want you, why the poor offer? You may decide to take it anyway. You are there to learn, to make a difference to the company, to help the CEO, whom presumably you like a lot. Understand that the big board seats go to people with contacts, not insight. What is insight compared with the ability to pick up the phone and get through?

I accept the offer and serve on the board for a year, until the company is folded into another of the CMGI companies. On the whole, a great experience.

And the rest of the best?

That is for you to suggest, in any and all categories relating to the soloist. Post your entries on:

www.ivillage.com/TheSoloist

Acknowledgements

The last secret I have to share is this: that a soloist who most proudly stands alone can only do so when she has mastered the art—and arc—of empathy. Praise independence, but unless you're interdependent, you're nothing. Even when you think you're alone, you've got to embrace all that mojo right beside you.

My mojo forces consisted of:

My agent, Sandy Dijkstra, who has been wise and guiding and available at odd hours and normal ones. Thanks also to her wonderful colleagues Sandra Zane, Clare Labram, and Rita Holm.

My editor, Lisa Berkowitz, vice president and director of marketing and communications at HarperCollins, has been a friend for years. Brilliant, spirited, Lisa is pure inspiration. Beneath that gorgeous blonde exterior is a gorgeous mind, heart and soul. Lisa: you're awesome!

Adrian Zackheim, publisher of Harper Business, was always my toughest competitor back when I was a publisher. Whenever agents and editors would extol him to me, I'd say, Oh you're exaggerating. I now realise they were underplaying his talents so as not to freak me out. I have proof that Adrian makes the impossible seem easy.

This book would not exist without George Gendron, editor of Inc., whose idea it was to begin a diary on soloing. George was the first to apply the term soloist to the class of individuals who were breaking rank with organisations of every kind. If the solo movement has a father, it is him.

Then there is the incomparable Alan Webber, cofounding editor with Bill Taylor of the terrific magazine *Fast Company*, whose many discussions with me on all things have been pure adrenalin.

Thanks to Bubba Levy, the model of understanding and generosity. To Della Silverman I owe important insights into living solo bravely.

Thanks also to Michael Hopkins of Inc., Jeff Seglin of Harvard, and Tracy Goss: teachers of the first order. And to Ethan Nelson, researcher par excellence.

And of course, Avram: mind of plenty, heart of wisdom, hero. Thoreau at Walden lived within the sound of his mother's dinner bell. I was never far from your call, always the sound of rescue, genius, laughter.

I'm a lucky soloist to have such friends and advisers, and wish I could offer them more than acknowledgments. But then each gave this soloist so much, they must already know the Czelaw Milosz poem:

> You received gifts from me; they were accepted. . . .
> The smell of winter apples, of hoarfrost, and of linen.
> There are nothing but gifts on this poor, poor Earth.

And there are nothing but givers in the life of the soloist.